... AND THE MYTH
OF LOST LANDS

Llys Helig
and the Myth of Lost Lands

by

Michael Senior

ISBN: 0-86381-767-X

Cover photo: Marcus Elliott
Cover design: Sian Parri

First published in 2002 by
Gwasg Carreg Gwalch, 12 Iard yr Orsaf, Llanrwst,
Wales LL26 0EH
℡ 01492 642031   ▤ 01492 641502
✆ books@carreg-gwalch.co.uk   website: www.carreg-gwalch.co.uk

Then listen, Socrates, to a tale which, though strange, is certainly true . . . I will tell an old-world story, which I heard from an old man . . .

Plato, *Critias*

Acknowledgements

In writing this book I have received the unstinting and unhesitating assistance of Nigel Bannerman and of Tom Parry, two current experts on the subject, and I wish to record my debt to their generosity with their information and their time.

I am grateful too to David Chapman and Marcus Elliott for sharing recollections of their trip to Llys Helig, and to the latter for supplying photographs; to David Ash and to Rhiannon Ash for the supply of documents; to Peter Welford for the loan of a book; and to the Librarians and staff of the County Libraries of Shropshire, and of Essex. As ever I am impressed by the efficiency of our own County Library system, and have again been glad of the helpfulness of its staff in Llandudno and Conwy.

Also I should like to thank Mary Meldrum for her help in correcting the proofs.

Contents

Preface

The house in which I was born, on the western beach of the Great Orme, *(Y Gogarth)*, in Llandudno, often felt endangered by the sea. On a bad day the spray from the breakers stung the bedroom windows. My father got so tired of losing part of his garden to each storm that he had a concrete breakwater constructed at great expense. The angry sea simply took it away. Parts of it were to be seen scattered in fragments half a mile away along Llandudno's West Shore. Undeterred, he built another one, better reinforced.

A short way up the coast near where we lived the ruins of a medieval bishop's palace lay in pieces on the foreshore, a reminder of the sea's ravenous appetite for land.

On a good day, when this monster had retreated or lay resting, I played happily in its territory. Sometimes the tide would disappear from sight, giving us miles of dry sand, just like land, but a different colour. There was no sign of the sea. One could walk right out into the bay. All the way out, we used to say, almost as far as Llys Helig.

Llys Helig lay somewhere on the horizon of my childhood, a mystery, and yet a landmark, somewhere out there. For me then it was both numinous and very real. That, I now find, sums it up. It has its roots in both worlds, that of fact and that of fancy, and whatever its identity 'really' is in the one of them, it will be counterparted by an equally real identity in the other.

The name means 'Helig's Court', and so seems at the outset to present us with a begged question. Because place-names are among our most ancient and durable artefacts, we have to take this designation seriously. How did it come by this name? What are the implications of it? What has it meant to people in the past – 'Helig's Court' – and, more to the point, what does it mean to us now? These are the sort of questions I shall be trying to answer in this book.

Llys Helig is the name of a group of rocks in Conwy Bay about a mile from the shore of Penmaenmawr. In explanation of the name, in the local tradition with which I grew up, it is said to be the ruins of the palace of a king called Helig whose lands formed what is now Conwy Bay.

Is that what it is? Or if not, what is it?

Much work has been done over a long period in the attempt to answer these questions. This book is both a summary of that work and an assessment of what, as a result of it, we now know about Llys Helig.

Introduction

SELECTIVE VISION

'These stones,' wrote William Ashton in 1920, 'did not vary six inches from a straight line . . . It is quite impossible for anyone to view these 350 or more yards of strictly rectangular remains and to entertain the slightest doubt as to their having been human handiwork.'

Quite impossible? 'The present writer,' records Dr F.J. North in 1940, 'feels confident that there is no regularity in the distribution of the stones that would support the view that they were walls . . . No walls could have been built with such a heterogeneous assemblage . . . ' His colleague, W.F. Grimes, who waded amongst them, says of the stones: 'If in spite of unsuitability and irregularity the stones had been found to occur in comparatively narrow banks or ridges, I should have been obliged to acknowledge the force of the argument for their artificial origin . . . I was left with the impression, not of a series of ridges which *might* have been ruined walls, but of an apparently unbroken mass of boulders which in some places were banked up higher than in others.'

Until recently (when a more scientific approach has prevailed) people went to look at Llys Helig in order to find what they had decided was there. Ashton went to find a ruined palace, North to show that it was no more than a geological feature. North showed how Ashton might have been deluded in his sighting of walls by a trick of his angle of vision; but North was there largely to discountenance Ashton.

There is perhaps a matter of fashion involved in this

dichotomy. By 1939, when North went, the (to us) slightly fey romanticism which influenced the early part of the century (Ashton's trip was made in 1908) had been severely reversed by a new spirit of scientific positivism.

We have to face the fact, I suppose, that today's spirit of scientific objectivity which I just referred to might be as much of an illusion as those previous visions, itself a sort of preconception which will lead us to see what we look for. What though, we may ask meanwhile, are the facts?

One fact is: here is a gathering of stones. The other fact, which draws our attention to this feature, is that there is a story.

I am going to deal in this book with the story first, and then the stones. The story at least does not suffer the disadvantage of lurking just out of sight beneath murky water. It is, as it happens, right out there in the forefront of our joint consciousness. It will soon be seen that it is a story we have known all our lives.

This will take us, geographically, quite a long way from Conwy Bay. The exile will not last for long, though. We will soon be coming back. When we do so I hope it will be with more insight into the background to the feature itself and so more chance to look at it clearly. The second half of the book focuses on the stones. It will take a close look at Llys Helig itself. It will take a close look, as well, at the succession of close looks at Llys Helig which have been taken already by others.

I The last banquet

Although the story of Helig has its roots in ancient lore, and
its written form derives from an account in the 17th century,
its full-blown expression belongs to the early and mid
nineteenth. It contains some details which appear to have
come from elsewhere, some which can be traced, and some
of which the remoter sources are not known; they probably
belong to a local oral tradition. The earliest guide-book to
Llandudno, for instance, that of 1849, tells the outline of the
story (the part for which we know the ultimate sources),
then adds:

> This inundation is still recorded in the traditional tales
> of the neighbourhood with the following additions: it
> had been prophesied, four generations previously,
> that vengeance would overtake the family of Helig ab
> Glanawg for the crimes of his ancestors. *Dial a ddaw,
> dial a ddaw,* was continually heard, although uttered by
> an invisible being. *Yn amser dy wyrion, neu dy orwyrion,*
> was the appointed time, and the inundation was so
> sudden that the servant, who, on going to the cellar to
> draw liquor, first observed the water, had only an
> opportunity of warning the harper of his danger,
> when all the others were overwhelmed by the flood in
> the midst of their festivities.

'Revenge is coming,' said the invisible voice. Clearly in a

better version of the story someone asked 'When?' 'In the time of your grandsons, or great-grandsons,' came the misleadingly reassuring reply. His grandsons and great-grandsons, however, were present at the fatal feast.

A notable feature here occurs, at the start of the developed story: it involved a spread of some seven generations. The calamity concerned the sins of Helig's ancestors, and had been foretold for four generations; it was to affect the third generation of his descendants too.

This emphasis on a number of generations will concern us again, when we come to discuss the matter of oral lore. In the meantime we may note that it can also be understood in the context of the Welsh concept *ach*, meaning pedigree or lineage, which in turn provides the basis of the notion of 'degrees of kinship' which govern (for instance) the rights to restitution for a wrong in *Cyfraith Hywel Dda* (the body of traditional Welsh law stemming from the edicts of the tenth-century king of that name, codified during the Middle Ages). It is because the law was based in this way that an almost obsessive concern with lineage dominated Welsh thinking. Sir John Rhys, for instance, in his late-Victorian work *Celtic Folklore*, puts it thus:

> In the case of the landed families of ancient Wales, every member of them had his position and liabilities settled by his pedigree, which had to be exactly recorded down to the eighth generation or eighth lifetime in Gwynedd, and to the seventh in Gwent and Dyfed. Those generations were reckoned the limits of recognised family relationship according to the Welsh Laws . . .

The crime, the curse, the complacency; the feast, the boy, the harpist; the rushing onset of doom, and the scarce survivors. These are archetypes then elaborated in the Victorian retellings of the story. North gives L.S. Costello's 1845 version, in the latter's guide *The Falls, Lakes, and Mountains of North Wales*, as a typical example, and we may I think take it as an early influence on others. Costello says the event was prophesied 'for generations' and that it was a punishment 'for the crimes of his ancestors'. He mentions the cry of *'Dial a ddaw'* by an invisible 'wailer'; he has some additional details about the fatal feast:

> . . . there was a great feast in the house of Helig, and the guests forgot, in their jovial carousal, that fate was only pausing to overtake them. They called for more wine, and a servant was despatched into the cellar to produce some, while the old harper sat leaning on his harp, and the tears ran down upon the strings, for his spirit foresaw some coming evil. They reproached him for his silence, and he put forth his hand to awaken the chords, when a cry struck his ear, and the next moment the servant who had gone for wine rushed wildly into the hall, shrieking – 'the tide! the tide!'
>
> Those two alone had time to quit the house of Helig, and found safety in the mountains; all besides were swallowed – lands, flocks, and villages – by the impetuous torrent; and the fertile vale of Conway for miles was all one sheet of foaming waters, as it remains to this day. At very low ebb, or with a strong south-west wind, waves may be distinctly seen breaking upon a causeway which runs into the sea at the Great Orme's Head; this is called the *Muriau*, or *the walls*.

The silent harpist and his tears, introduced here, make a comeback in John Hicklin's version, in *The Handbook of Llandudno*, of 1858, for which Costello is the evident source. The causeway at the Great Orme's Head, however, is never repeated, and may have been recognised as a mistake for the location of Llys Helig. Hicklin however adds his own interesting variation: he says that 'Cantre'r Gwaelod' was the name of the fertile vale which once occupied the area of Conwy Bay. ' . . . extending from Bangor Fawr to Gogarth, and in breadth from Dwygyfylchi (near Penmaen Bach) to the point of Flintshire . . . ' The story of the inundation of Cantre'r Gwaelod, traditionally supposed to be a tract of land now under water in Cardigan Bay, is so closely related to that of Llys Helig, and so often confused with it, that we cannot entirely treat it as a separate subject. We shall have to investigate both the other story and its connection with ours in more detail, but it can be said at once that in its form as usually conveyed – and later we shall investigate the authenticity of this – it is supposed to concern the area of Aberdyfi. At the very least it can be said that Hicklin appears to have access to another source, as well as to Costello.

Hicklin then quotes Costello verbatim, though without naming his source. He goes on to cite more explicitly what is probably one of the first modern attempts to investigate the connection of the legend with the stones. Pugh's *Cambria Depicta, a Tour through North Wales*, was published in 1816. Pugh says little, however, about the story – 'we floated over the place where, tradition says, one Helig ab Glanog, a chieftain of the sixth century, had great possessions, extending far into this bay; but which were suddenly overwhelmed by the sea . . . ' Pugh's account of his trip will concern us later, when we come to look at the stones.

One thing that is striking about the various 19th century versions of the story is that they do not begin with the feast and the disaster, or even with the curse, the warning, or the remote and unspecified crimes. They begin with a hillock called Trwyn-yr-Wylfa, which they translate as 'The Point of the Place of Wailing'; and in doing so they reveal their ultimate source.

'An Ancient Survey of Penmaenmawr', supposed to have been written by Sir John Wynn of Gwydir in the first half of the 17th century, is in fact, even when they are unaware of this, the basic provenance for much of the information which later writers give about Llys Helig. This in fact is the hinge between the ancient traditional material and the modern development of the story, and of such importance is it that we shall be giving it more detailed attention.

The writer of the 'Ancient Survey' starts this part of the story with some words about Helig and the pre-inundation geography of this coast. The river Ell ran through fruitful and pleasant vales:

> most of them beynge the land of Helig ap Glannog, whose chieffest pallace stood in this vale muche about the mydle way from Penmen Mawer to Gogarth (in Englishe Armes Head) the ruynes whereof is now to bee seene uppon a grownd ebbe some two myles within the sea directly over against Trevyn yr Wylva, which is a hill leynge in the myddyst of the parishe of Dwygyfylchi within the landes of Sir John Bodnel knight, unto which hyll Helyg ap Glanno and his people did runn upp to save themsealves, beynge endaungered with the sudden breakynge in of the sea uppon them, and there saved there lyves; and beynge come upp to the poynte of that hill, and lookynge

backe and behouldynge that dreadfull and ruthfull spectacle which they hadd to survay and looke uppon, insteade of there incomparable vale which did abound in fruytfullnes and excell all other vales in this parte of England in all fertility and plentifullness, Helig ap Glannog and all his people, wryngynge there handes together, made a greate outcry bewaylinge their misfortune and callyng unto God for mercy, the poynt of which hill to this day is called Trwyn (r) Wylfa, that is to say the poynt of the dolefull hill or the mowrnynge hill. . .

A problem at once arises for those who wish the story to have the traditional ingredient of the few survivors (two in this case, but often, we shall see, only one). Helig *and all his people* went up onto Trwyn yr Wylfa, looked back over the water covering their land, and wept. The writer of the 1849 guide, for instance, has the story ending with the servant and the harper escaping, 'when all the others were overwhelmed by the flood . . . ' yet has just said that Trwyn-yr-Wylfa got its name because 'it was to this place that the inhabitants with difficulty escaped, so sudden and overwhelming was the inundation'. The whole lot of them, apparently. Certainly enough to give the place its name.

Later guide-books followed this format, adding their own variants. The 1934-5 Ward Lock guide, for instance, 'Llandudno and North Wales', has an imported angle on the story, but retains the centrality of 'Trwyn-y-Wylfa'. A high-born maiden was told by a bard that she could not marry into a house at discord with hers 'until eels came of their own accord to her father's cellar'.

But one day there was a sudden inrush of the sea over

the smiling land, and only with great difficulty did the maiden escape to higher ground. Some say that she alone was saved; others that some of her relatives escaped also. By reason of that flood a bold projecting spur midway in the vale bears the name of Trwyn-y-Wylfa, or the *Weeping Point*. At very low tides it is possible to step from a boat on to the ruins of the ancient mansion, known as *Llys Helig*.

It is in fact almost as if the writers were arguing backwards from the name of the outcrop to the legend: it is called 'the point of wailing', and that requires an explanation.

North, as usual, is not disposed to let people get away with any error, and firmly puts us right on the meaning of the name, in the process relentlessly undermining long-held folk tradition and the passage of conventional wisdom over the ages – all, he points out, derived from the booklet attributed to Wynn. (His calling it 'Notes' will shortly be explained.)

It would seem that the author of the *Notes* had allowed his ingenuity to outrun his knowledge of Welsh. *Trwyn yr Wylfa* means 'The Point or promontory of the look-out', for *Wylfa* is a mutation of *gwylfa*, derived from *gwylio* (to watch) and has nothing to do with *wylo* (to weep) or *wylofain* (to lament).

It is of course an excellent place for a look-out, commanding as it does the mouth of the Sychnant Pass, the coastal plain, and the seaward approaches. It has an unexpectedly broad plateau near its top, suitable as a site for keeping watch, or indeed for wailing. From there one can see the bay and its limestone headlands, Penmon and Puffin *(Ynys Seiriol)*, and the Orme, the sea's textured surface lined by the meandering currents of apparent underwater streams.

Sometimes perverse, sometimes in irritable temper, it is often bland, though wearing a Mona Lisa smile. Try and find out about me, those curving waterways and dimpled sheens suggest; as if knowing that, though tempted to try, we never will.

Using a powerful-enough imagination one can just about make out, among the shadows on its opaque surface, an underlying pattern of gentle undulation, and elusive as ever in the distant haze, a darker mark which might perhaps be the upward shadow of Llys Helig.

II Notes to be observed

Dr F.J. North was a distinguished geologist who for a long time held the post of 'Keeper of the Department of Geology' at the National Museum of Wales in Cardiff. He contributed the section on 'Geology and the Physical Background' to *Snowdonia*, the book which records the state of the new National Park, published in 1949. Already by the late 30's he was a popular lecturer, and as such he came on more than one occasion to address the 'Llandudno, Colwyn Bay and District Field Club'. In 1936 he gave them a talk on 'The Scenery of the Welsh Coast'. In doing this, he later said, 'whilst discussing local changes involving encroachment of the sea it became necessary to mention the legend of Llys Helig'. He said that in doing so he intended to do no more than strip away the ivy from the old ruins of the legend so that the story might be more plainly seen. ' . . . but a newspaper report of the occasion gleefully credited me with having "debunked" and old Welsh legend.'

> Nothing had been farther from my mind, for destructive criticism, as unprofitable as it is easy, serves no useful purpose . . . I had not set out to destroy a legend but to discover when and how it came into being.

This was not however what seemed to *The North Wales Weekly News* to have happened when in due course North, now having visited the site, presented his findings. The picturesque legend of the inundation and the belief that the rocks were the remains of Helig's palace had been 'thoroughly discredited', it said.

> On Thursday evening at the Llandudno Public Library members of the Llandudno and Colwyn Bay Field Club heard Dr North literally put 'finis' to the legend. Dr North . . . declare(d) emphatically that there was not a shred of evidence to prove that the weed-covered rocks which were inspected by the expedition on August 17th last could have been the remains of any kind of building.

The expedition of August 17th, 1939 (of which more later) had been organised as a result of the feeling of dissatisfaction arising from the 1936 talk. North's suggestions were, he wrote, 'not acceptable to those who had come to regard the story as history, and they were challenged by members of the Llandudno and Colwyn Bay Field Club who had actually visited Llys Helig and who could speak from personal knowledge of the stones'. North at the time could not, and they invited him 'to join an expedition to examine the site', no doubt hoping that the evidence of his eyes would dispel his scepticism. To their dismay it did the opposite.

North's findings, together with a report by the archaeologist W.F. Grimes, an adviser to the Ordnance Survey Department, were published as 'A Supplement to the Proceedings' of the Field Club in 1940. This influential work lies in the background of much of the discussion in this book. It must be said at this point that there has been a recent reaction in fashion surrounding this subject, and current experts on Llys Helig and the coastline (such as my respected friend Nigel Bannerman) dismiss much of North's findings as being angled and unfairly weighted – much as North himself dismisses the work of Ashton and others. I do not know, at this stage, whether these views are another example of how a certain programme leads to an interpretation of the evidence: or whether one party is right, and the other wrong. All one can do for the time being is identify and report exactly what they each see the evidence to be.

For a specialist in geology North has a surprisingly academic and penetrating approach to literary history. In fact nine-tenths of his paper, 'The Legend of Llys Helig – its origins and significance', deal with the literary and historical background, followed by a few pages of geology.

The first part of North's paper takes the booklet usually known as 'An Ancient Survey of Pen Maen Mawr', said to be by Sir John Wynn of Gwydir, and by careful analysis of its origins shows that it is not correctly a book called that at all, but someone's notes on such a book, and that it is probably not by Sir John Wynn. 'If the original manuscript exists its present resting place is unknown,' he wrote, and spent much time comparing copies. The timing was unfortunate. Shortly after the Field Club published North's work the original manuscript turned up, towards the end of 1940, during an exercise of recataloguing, in the National Library of Wales (where it had been, when North thought it was lost), among papers formerly belonging to Edward Breese of Porthmadog and later to E.H. Owen of Tŷ Coch, Caernarfon. It is listed as MS 820D.

That this is the original is evidenced not just from its distinctly 17th century style but from the fact that alterations and additions, made in the same hand as the text, are those such as would be made by the author himself in the course of writing the piece and not by a copyist. Internal evidence (references to John Williams as being Bishop of Lincoln and Lord Keeper) date it securely to between 1621 and 1625, in other words during the lifetime of Sir John Wynn. Yet it is not by him. We have enough of his authenticated writing. It is not in his hand.

North had come near to this conclusion on other evidence even before knowing of the manuscript (though he thought that Wynn might have been involved). The attribution of the booklet to Wynn first occurs in the 1722 edition of Camden's *Britannia* in a marginal note, amplifying with the words 'Sir John Wyn of Gudyr' a reference in the 1695 edition (in additional notes by Edward Lhuyd quoting parts of the 'survey') to the author as 'a person of quality of the reign of Charles I'.

In the original and the early copies the work is headed 'Notes to be observed before you lett your survey passe your handes'. It did not come to be called by its present title until it was printed and published in 1859 by J.O. Halliwell, copied, he said, from a manuscript owned by Thomas Wright. Halliwell claimed to be making a true copy of this, so perhaps it was Wright who coined the title – wo do not have this manuscript, unless indeed it is the one referred to above. It seems unlikely that this was the title of the Wright manuscript, since there is little in the way of survey and not much about Penmaenmawr in the work, as we shall see. But then we may equally wonder why Halliwell chose to call it this.

To return to North's paper, after discussing the 'Notes' and their authorship and origins, he then turns to an investigation of the history of the legend itself, both in its relatively recent developed form, as we have done in

Chapter I, and its ancient origins, which will concern us in Chapter III. He relates the story to that of Cantre'r Gwaelod, an inevitable comparison which throws up some interesting parallels. A section interposed in this discussion, 'The subsidences to which the legends relate', considers the geological conditions which display coastal change. That too will concern us again, but it must be said that North is not concerned, as is sometimes thought, to show that the legend is pure fallacy or fiction, but to suggest that the literal interpretation of it – that the stones are the ruins of buildings which were submerged in the 6th century – is impossible. It is this which has led him to be classed (to use his own term) as iconoclastic. Many of us (as Nigel Bannerman has himself said to me) grew up believing that the North version, as so interpreted, was the end of the matter. Yet a closer reading of him does not show him to be the reductionist which he might, taking this one point, appear. He simply rejected the time-scale. It cannot have been a Dark Age inundation that is referred to by the story; it could he argues have been one in the Neolithic or Bronze Age. Nevertheless, because the flooding must have taken place so long ago, he does dismiss the idea of a man-made nature for the stone remains. They are natural geological features, but they were submerged, albeit a very long time ago – but not so long that human habitations would not also have been affected by the same events.

North returned to the subject in 1955 with the publication of a book called *Sunken Cities – Some legends of the coast and lakes of Wales*, published by the University of Wales Press. It is there that he says that it all arose from the Llandudno lecture, of which a newspaper report "gleefully credited me with having 'debunked' an old Welsh legend".

Between the original paper and *Sunken Cities* North had

written about 'the Evolutions of the Bristol channel', and also the evidence of finds in Paviland Cave, on the Gower, for drowned lands off the coast. *Sunken Cities* repeats and expands on much of the discussion of the first work, adds some lake stories and another North Wales coast one, that of Caer Arianrhod (which is not, however, an indundation story), and brings to the task his expanded knowledge of coastal change – and his awareness of the formerly missing manuscript of 'Notes to be observed'.

Knowing now that this work was not by Sir John Wynn it is easier for him, and us, to see it in its true light. It is not, as was anyway clear, a survey, but somebody's commentary addressed to somebody else who had written such a work, which is anyway what it says. The first part of it, amounting to more than half the whole, consists of a set of pedigrees tracing Helig's descent from Cunedda, in which he tells the story of Helig's flooded lands:

> This Helig ap Glannog was lord of Abergele Rhos, Arllechwedd, Llŷn, Cantregwaylod and Earle of Herefford. In his tyme happened the greate inundacion which surrounded Cantred Gwayloi and the most delicate fruytfulle and pleasant vale leynge from Bangor vawr yn gwynedd to Gogarth and soe to Tyganwy or Gannog Castle, in leangth and in breadthe from Dwygyfylchi to the poynte of Flyntshire, which came upp from Ruthlan to Priestholme . . .

Some of this of course is nonsense – it does not need anyone as eagle-eyed as North to point out that the Earldom of Hereford was not created until 1067, and it is difficult to see how anyone knowledgeable in the history of North Wales

26

could include this as one of Helig's titles, even by way of a misreading. Of interest to us is the association of Helig with Cantre'r Gwaelod. This does not say, we should note, that Helig's lands and Cantre'r Gwaelod were the same place (although he was lord of them both, and much more), but in fact that the inundation affected both Cantre'r Gwaelod *and* the fruitful vale between Bangor and Gogarth, which is the one where he then locates Helig, in the passage about the river Ell which we have quoted in the previous chapter. The same inundation in fact, he says, affected the whole of the North Wales coast. The flood which 'surrounded' Cantre'r Gwaelod also 'did surround many other riche and fruytfulle bottomes and vales within the countyes of Carnarvon, Flynt, Anglesey and Merionudd, most of them beynge the land of Helig ap Glannog, whose chieffest pallace stood in this vale muche about the mydle way from Penmen Mawer to Gogarth . . . ' As we may judge by the host of titles he is given at the start, Helig was thought by this writer to have been the lord of most of North Wales; it was just his *chiefest* palace that stood in Conwy Bay.

It must be said that before he continues with his pedigrees the writer of the Notes displays some further ignorance: he credits Helig with a palace at Pwllheli on the basis that the name is short for 'Pwllhelig', whereas of course it comes from 'pwll' *(pool)* and 'heli', and means 'sea-water pool'; he thinks Traeth Mawr is so called after the river Mawr, whereas only a little Welsh (and a little common sense) would inform him that it simply means 'big', and is contrasted with Traeth Bach. The river of course is not called Mawr. It is the Glaslyn that runs through Traeth Mawr, as Sir John Wynn perfectly well knew. If it were he to whom these Notes were addressed, we can imagine him at this point straining to control his famous temper.

Having made Helig central to this theme, fifth in line of descent from Cunedda, and explained his importance to us, the writer then traces his descent, to 'moste of the pryme men within the country of Caernarvon'; several pages of lineage in fact then follow, showing how the holders of land in North Wales are descended from Helig, among them John Williams of Cochwillan, the Lord Keeper.

Three of Helig's sons, we are told, became saints; and Seiriol, the founder of the monastery on Priestholme (Puffin Island now, but still *Ynys Seiriol* in Welsh), was his brother. He had, the writer says, a hermitage at Penmaenmawr, and built a causeway from there to the island 'whereuppon hee might walke drye from his church att Priestholme to his chappell att Penmen Mawre, the vale beying very lowe grownd and wette, which pavemt may att this day bee discerned from Penmen Mawre to Priestholme when the sea is cleere, yf a man liste to goe in a bote to see ytt'. Evidently this was before the inundation, since after that we are told that Seiriol had a road made around Penmaenmawr headland; but then this low wet ground does not sound like the same place as the rich and fruitful vales of a few pages earlier, and indeed it is tempting to see the flood as a gradual process, hundreds if not thousands of years of increasing wetness, and so only allegorically attached to the lifetimes of Helig and Seiriol, and the times of churches and saints.

The writer of the Notes goes on about the road around the headland, which was a problem in the 17th century and subsequently, which he says was 'kepte and repayred by a heremyte'. There then occurs a remarkable and famous passage, which will concern us again, indeed more than once:

In this greate washe uppon a lowe ground ebbe, in every March and June, when ytt ebbes farthest, are to be seen the rootes of greate oake and ashe att the furthest ebbe att all but onely uppon spring tydes in March and August; this I speake as an eye wittness, havynge seene the rootes my sealf and taken them upp, soe that ytt shoulde seeme that this vale before the inundacion was a woodland countrey.

The correct months are March and August; in the manuscript June is crossed out in the second instance and August written above it – evidently he missed the error in the paragraph's first line, and copyists have also retained it, causing much confusion. The tree roots, for their part, are still there.

It is then that the only part of the work which could justify its modern title occurs: a survey of the antiquities of Penmaenmawr. He gives us a useful view of the fort at Braich y Dinas (the accuracy of which Pennant later confirms), useful because this has now been completely destroyed by quarrying. He describes the circle of standing stones known to us as The Druids' Circle. Interestingly he shows an attitude to this completely at contrast with our own. We now tend to see all unexplained artefacts (completely without justification) as being religious in nature. This 17th century gentleman of quality sees them as being recreational or military:

Ytt shoulde seeme that this was a place whereunto the ancient Brittaynes came from the Dinas aforesaid to encampe themsealves and trayne there souldiers; ytt standes in a place fytte for justes and turnamentes, and this cyrcle thus rounded with these longe stones might

> bee the place where the kinges tente was pitched: and neer to this circle there are three pretty bigg stones uppon there endes standynge triangle wiese lieke a tribbett, whereuppon as they say was sett a greate cauldron to boyle meate in . . .

He did not know, of course, that more than two thousand years separated the hillfort from the stone circle. But to a large extent he speaks for us as well as himself when he says 'ytt is greate pitty that our Brittishe histories are soe ymbeseled that wee have noe certtaynty for these things, but must onely rely uppon tradicion'.

It is noteworthy that in spite of the writer's consciousness of having to rely on 'tradicion' and speculation regarding the hillfort and the standing stones, he earlier reports Helig's lands, palace and disaster as being undisputed fact. Not 'it is said', but 'whose chieffest palace stood in this vale . . . the ruynes whereof is now to bee seene uppon a grownd ebbe . . .'

Towards the end of his little book the writer's purpose becomes clearer. Much of the time he appears to have been adding information from his own knowledge, of genealogy and antiquity, to that of someone else. Now he makes two corrections. The writer of the 'survey' has evidently said that Deganwy castle was built by the earls of Chester. He is firmly put right on that: 'As for Tyganwy or Gannocke Castle, ytt was from the begynninge the chieffe seat of the King of Northwales, and not originally founded by any of the Earles of Chester . . . ' A detailed history to illustrate this fact then follows. 'This I have expressed to make ytt appeare that Tyganwy al's Gannocke Castell was an ancient Brittishe fortifficacion in the tyme of the Kinges of Brittayne . . . Once you may see ytt reediffied in Kinge Johns tyme to the Kinges use by the earle of Chester, but the castell was not originally buylte by any one of the earles of Chester.' He had, perhaps, been reading 'The Historie of Cambria, now called Wales', a book based on Humphrey Llwyd's translation of *Brut y Tywysogion*, the Welsh equivalent of the Anglo-Saxon Chronicle, published by David Powel, a Ruabon man, in 1584.

Similarly the writer being addressed seems to have said that the abbey at Bangor was first burnt down by Owain Glyndŵr. Our commentator knows that it had already been burnt by King John. Here the relationship between the two is explicit: one is addressing the other and making comments and corrections. 'Whereas you say that Bangor Vawr was destroyed by Owen Glynndwr in revenge of Bushoppe Madogs treason, true ytt ys that the Cathedrall churche, and Bangor house with the relickes of Bangor fyred by Glyndwr . . . but Bangor Vawr was formerly in anno 1212 burned by Kinge John, and Buppe Robert taken perforce, who was afterwarde ransomed for 200 hawkes.'

That Wynn was somehow involved in this exchange is perhaps hinted at by two internal clues. During the Llys Helig passage and in the family trees Sir John Bodvel is mentioned by name, and he was Wynn's son-in-law – hence his pedigree important. Similarly important is that of John Williams, the Lord Keeper, since Wynn's son Owen was at the time hoping to marry Williams' niece – and sure enough some lines of pedigree are found to end in him: 'But from a daughter you shall fynd that the right Reverend and Ryght ho: John bisshopp of Lincolne, lord keeper of his Majestries greate seale of England . . . is descended from Madog ap Jarddur . . . ' Nevertheless it may confidently be said that it was not Sir John Wynn of Gwydir who knew where to look for the ruins of Llys Helig, who misunderstood the meaning of Trwyn y Wylfa, who took a boat to see Sarn Seiriol at low tide, and who had been on that beach when the tree stumps were revealed, and indeed had the utmost empirical knowledge of these, since he had taken them up.

Who it was we do not know. North speculates in his paper that it might have been Sir Thomas ap Williams, a friend, relative and literary colleague of Wynn's who had helped him compile the *History of the Gwydir Family* and was involved with Sir John in producing a Welsh-Latin dictionary. But the discovery of the manuscript spoilt this theory, since it is not in Williams' hand either. Nor is there any point in speculating, as some have done, that although Wynn did not physically write the work he dictated the notes to someone else, since that would still leave the problem of whom he was addressing – the phrasing of the corrections shows that it cannot have been himself. In any case he was a copious writer, and does not seem to have found the need to dictate.

Whoever it was by, we have to thank, and to blame, the work known as the 'Ancient Survey' for much of our received opinion of Llys Helig. It is one of the earliest and most unequivocal recordings of the story. Of crucial important to us here is that it is the one which relates the story to the stones.

III Elffin goes fishing

The earliest mentions of Helig, occurring in a collection of genealogical lists known as *Bonedd y Saint*, written in the early 13th century and surviving in the form of a manuscript known as Peniarth No. 16, do not say where his drowned lands were. ' . . . helic voel. odyno helic. gwyr heuyt a oresgynnwys mor eu tir.' Helig Foel, that is, of Dyno Helig, whose lands were overwhelmed by the sea. This is clear enough, but a confusion of location sets in when this simple early form of the story gets transcribed. In one of the manuscripts collected by Iolo Morganwg we read of 'Helig the son of Glannog of the plain of Gwyddno, whose territory was overwhelmed by the sea'. There are good reasons for not trusting the Iolo manuscripts, but it is interesting that Peniarth No 16 (which mentions Helig) also bears a reference to Gwyddno as a place, rather than, as the name came to mean, a king. Here Seithenyn, later Gwyddno's henchman, is the king: 'Seithenin, Vrenhin o vaes gwydno . . . ' Seithenyn, king of Maes Gwyddno.

The source similarly says of Seithenyn, as of Helig, that his land was overwhelmed by the sea. It might thus have been the same land, or neighbouring. We could assume that the two figures were affected by one inundation, but the context does not tell us where: North says that the author of the 'Notes' (as he calls the 'Ancient Survey') 'might have suggested that the lands which Helig lost were adjacent to those of Seithenyn had he not been so much engrossed with the northern coastal regions'. This is to some extent to beg the question – it assumes we have good reason for placing Seithenyn further south! – and it could in fact be put the other way round: writers who place Maes Gwyddno in Cardigan Bay *(Bae Ceredigion)* might have assumed that Seithenyn's land was adjacent to Helig's, in Conwy Bay, had they not been fixated on the southern location.

The story of Seithenyn and Gwyddno is to be found in the Triads, but since these (in their later form) issued from the library of Iolo Morganwg, we may imagine that the information therein derived from Iolo's imagination and so dates no further back than the 18th century. It is perhaps appropriate, for the sake of those unfamiliar with the intricacies of Welsh literary history, to explain why this is so.

Edward Williams was a poet and antiquarian, born in Glamorganshire in 1747, who took the bardic name of Iolo Morganwg, by which he is always known. He was a stonemason by trade, a laudanum addict most of his life; and an enthusiastic participant in the 18th century antiquarian revival. In the 1770's and 1790's he introduced a form of neo-Druidism to the London Welsh Society which developed into the Gorsedd; and his big achievement came with the acceptance of this as part of the annual eisteddfod ritual, at the Eisteddfod at the Ivy Bush, Carmarthen *(Caerfyrddin)*, in 1819.

In support of his conviction that Welsh tradition stretched unbroken back to the Druids, and so to the pre-Saxon island, 'he was prepared' (as Meic Stephens somewhat defensively puts it, in his invaluable *Oxford Companion to the Literature of Wales*) 'to exercise a fertile imagination and his considerable literary gifts, even to falsify the sources of Welsh history and to mislead his contemporaries . . . with the result that many scholars laboured throughout the nineteenth century under misapprehensions for which Iolo had been responsible'.

Doubts were beginning to be expressed early in the 1920's, by, for instance, John Morris-Jones, Professor of Welsh at Bangor University; but it was not until 1926, when the Iolo archive became lodged with the National Library and the literary historian G.J. Williams (whose life's work the disentanglement then became) was appointed to examine it, that the extent of the damage became clear. From about 1926, when Williams' conclusions were published, Iolo is ultimately exposed as a fabricator and forger.

The tantalising element is that we do not know to what extent Iolo, in making stories up, was using his knowledge of a genuine tradition, as did later retellers of Celtic lore. In many cases what Iolo gives us is supported by older and authenticated material. In this case, for instance, the entry for Seithenyn in the Triads is based on his occurrence in a publication of the 16th century. At the very least we may say that the developed story of Seithenyn and Cantre'r Gwaelod *(Gwyddno's kingdom)* comes now from the entry in Iolo's version of the Triads, published in 1801.

. . . the drunken Seithenin, son of Seithyn Said a king of Dimetia, who in his drunkenness let the sea over the hundred of Gwaelod so that all the houses and land which were there, were lost; where before that event sixteen fortified towns were reckoned there, superior to all the towns and fortified stations in Cambria, with the exception of Caerlion upon Usk. The hundred of Gwaelod was the dominion of Gwydnaw Garanhir, king of Cardigan. This event happened in the time of Ambrosius. The people who escaped from that inundation landed in Ardudwy, and the country of

Arvon, and the mountains of Snowdon, and other
places, which had not been inhabited before that
period.

We have several bits of information here, which have
formed the pattern of the usual version of the story.
Seithenyn is associated with the kingdom of Dimetia, that is:
Pembrokeshire. The extensive hundred of Gwaelod (the
'lowest' hundred) was ruled by the king of Cardigan, and so
is located in Cardigan Bay, as is also evidenced by its
displaced inhabitants arriving in Ardudwy – the area
around Harlech. The identification with the 'time of
Ambrosius' puts us in the late fifth century.

The *White Book of Rhydderch* version of the Triads, that is,
a mid-14th century version, does mention Gwyddno in
passing – one of the 'Three Golden Corpses' was that of
'Rhufawn the Radiant, son of Gwyddno' – and a late 16th
century appendix to the Triads gives his 'Hamper' – an item
also mentioned in the *Mabinogion* story 'Culhwch and
Olwen', possibly first written down in the 10th century, and
like other *Mabinogion* stories extant in 14th century
manuscript form – as one of the 'Three Treasures of the Isle
of Britain'; but none of the other events mentioned in the
later copy of the Triads occurs. There is no mention of
Seithenyn, nothing about Cantre'r Gwaelod, drunkenness, or
drowned lands.

Remarkably in the same story there is a reference to
someone named as 'Teithi the Old son of Gwynnan', which
is clearly connected to our material since it goes on: 'whose
dominions the sea overran, and with difficulty he himself
escaped . . . ' F.J. North shows convincingly that 'Teithi Hen'
(the old) could be a mistranscription of Seithenyn. It is not
uncommon, he says, for copyists to transcribe an 'S' as a 'T',

and an 'n' as an 'h'.

There is evidence (from two other references in the *White Book*) that Gwyddno was originally a northern figure, imported into our area, in which case he may somehow have replaced Helig as the protagonist of the story. Helig himself appears in what seems to have been a 'Triad' which strayed from the collection, and got recorded in the 13th century Exeter *Chonica de Wallia*, in which of the three kingdoms which the sea destroyed 'The second kingdom was that of Helig son of Glannog, it was between Cardigan and Bardsey, and as far as St David's . . . it lay from the mouth (Aberystwyth?) to Llŷn, and up to Aberdovey'. This evidence of an old tradition locating both Helig and the drowned land in Cardigan Bay only serves to emphasise the essential ambiguity of the whole matter. As Rachel Bromwich concludes, of the rival Cardigan and Conwy locations, in her paper on the subject in *The Early Cultures of North West Europe*: 'The stories have certainly influenced each other at some point, though it is not possible to point to one or other as the original.'

That there is a genuine tradition concerning the other elements so far missing, such as Seithenyn and drunkenness, is not in doubt. For once both Ashton and North are agreed: the earliest version of the story is a reference in a poem to be found in the *Black Book of Carmarthen*, which dates it to about 1200. It seems that Sir John Lloyd himself, the revered historian, told Ashton this: 'The writer is informed by Prof. J.E. Lloyd that the tradition cannot be traced further back than about 1200 A.D. . . . ' 'Seithenyn' is there admonished to face the foaming sea, which has covered the plain of Gwyddno.

There is no suggestion in the poem itself however that it is Seithenyn's fault, let alone that he was drunk. It was a maiden *('morvin')* who let loose well water (presumably, as in other stories, by failing to put the cover back on). A possible reference to drunkenness occurs, but on her part rather than his:

Seithenhin sawde allan.
ac edryuirde varanresmor.
maesguitnev rytoes.

Boed emendiceid y morvin
aeheligaut cvin.
finaun wenestir mor terruin.

Looseley following Sir John Rhys' translation, this seems to mean something like: Stand forth Seithenyn, and see the ranks of the waves covering Gwyddno's meadow. The maiden is cursed who loosed it after supping, the well-attendant of the governing sea.

What exactly this means is probably lost during the course of many transcriptions, but it appears to have something definitely to do with wells. Indeed Sir John Rhys, in his magisterial *Celtic Folklore*, points out that Welsh inundation stories were originally tales of the overflowing of wells, and only subsequently appear to have become (in some cases) coastal.

Such is the story of Bala lake *(Llyn Tegid)* in a version which Rhys was told by someone who had found it in a book published in 1889 but drawn from the collection of David Jones, of Trefriw, a mid-18th century poet.

In 1735 I had a conversation with a man concerning Tegid Lake. He had heard from old people that near the middle of it there was a well . . . and at that time the town was round about the well. It was obligatory to place a lid on the well every night . . . But one night it was forgotten, and by the morning, behold the town had subsided and the lake became three miles long and one mile wide. They say, moreover, that on clear days some people see the chimneys of the houses.

Rhys tells another version of the Bala story, and so similar is this in structure to the stories of the coastal plains that we may wonder which is borrowing from which. Here is the version Rhys gives, which he took from a book by Hugh Humphreys called *Llyfr Gwybodaeth Gyffredinol*, published in Caernarfon (he does not say when).

Tradition relates that Bala Lake is but the watery tomb of palaces of iniquity; and that some old boatmen can on quiet moonlight nights in harvest see towers in ruins at the bottom of its waters, and also hear at times a feeble voice saying, *Dial a ddaw, dial a ddaw*, (vengeance will come); and another voice inquiring, *Pa bryd y daw* (when will it come?). Then the first voice answers, *Yn y drydedd genhedlaeth* (in the third generation).

The voices were an echo of the past: the palaces had been inhabited by a cruel and oppressive prince, who

used frequently to hear a voice saying, 'Vengeance will come'. But he always laughed the threat away with reckless contempt.

A harper from the village is summoned to play at a great celebration at the birth of a grandchild. About midnight he is led out of the palace by a small bird whispering 'Vengeance, vengeance!' He is led to the top of a hill, where he spends the night.

> In the morning, as he turned his eyes in the direction of the palace, he could see no trace of it: the whole tract below was one calm, large lake, with his harp floating on the face of the waters.

Bala lake is called Llyn Tegid after Tegid Foel *(the Bald)*, a character who occurs at the start of the tale of Taliesin, (the provenance of which we shall shortly be discussing), with the interesting comment that his patrimony 'was the body of water that is known today as Llyn Tegid'. We saw at the start of this chapter that the earliest mention of Helig calls him 'Helig voel' (now spelt *foel*). Since the two inundation stories, Bala's and Llys Helig's, seem to be substantially the same, we may wonder if these are the same man, although there is no clear route by which either 'Tegid' or 'Helig' could be misreadings of the other.

Sir John gives other instances in which a well was supposed to have overflowed and formed a lake, such as that of Glasfryn, the Williams-Ellis property on the Llŷn peninsula, where somebody once forgot to close the door of a well, and again of lakes that have arisen from wells through human error, or come into being as a punishment for immediate, or ancestral, sins.

Gwyddno, for his part, now a king, appears in another apparently respectable source, the story of Taliesin, which occurs in some editions of *The Mabinogion*, the main collection of traditional Welsh material. The reason it does not occur in all editions is that it is not in either of the two 14th century manuscripts from which Gwyn Jones and

Thomas Jones drew their definitive version of the collection of stories, *The Red Book of Hergest*, or *The White Book of Rhydderch*. Lady Charlotte Guest, in her original edition, drew it from assorted sources, since there was no standard text; Patrick K. Ford uses a variation, in his 1977 Californian edition, which differs in several instances (sometimes crucially) from Lady Charlotte's. Here, first, is her introduction of Gwyddno:

> And at that time the weir of Gwyddno was on the strand between Dyvi and Aberystwyth, near to his own castle, and the value of a hundred pounds was taken in that weir every May eve. And in those days Gwyddno had an only son named Elphin, the most hapless of youths, and the most needy.

Here is Ford's:

> Also in that time there lived a wealthy squire near Caer Deganwy, and the story says he was called Gwyddno Garanhir (he was a lord). The text says he had a weir on the shore of the Conway adjacent to the sea, in which was caught as much as ten pounds worth of salmon every eve of All Hallows. The tale also says that Gwyddno had a son called Elphin son of Gwyddno, who was in service in the court of King Maelgwn.

Apart from the focus on the weir, there is little in common between these accounts. Above all the shift of location from Cardigan Bay to Conwy Bay must strike us, and the identification of the time as being that of Maelgwn, the mid sixth century. Commenting on her sources, and admitting

41

the inadequacy of them, Lady Charlotte says:

> No perfect copy of the Mabinogi of Taliesin being accessible, it has been necessary to print it in the present series from two fragments. The former of the two is contained in a MS. in the Library of the Welsh School in London. It is written in a modern round hand, and bears the title 'Y Prif-feirdd Cymreig, sef Canau &c. a gasglwyd ganwyf fi, William Morris o Gaergybi ym Môn. 1758'. The MS. is of quarto size.
>
> The second fragment is from a MS. in the library of the late Iolo Morganwg, and was kindly communicated by his son . . .

The Cambridge 'History of English Literature' comments on Lady Charlotte's sources:

> All the tales translated by Lady Guest are taken from *The Red Book of Hergest*, with the exception of *The History of Taliesin*. *Taliesin*, in the form we have it, is a compilation of obviously late medieval origin, and is not found in any MS of an earlier date than the end of the sixteenth century.

Professor Patrick K. Ford, Associate Professor of English and Celtic Studies at the University of California, Los Angeles, translated and edited *The Mabinogion and other Medieval Welsh Tales*, published by the University of California Press at Berkeley, in 1977. He is explicit on his sources for *The Tale of Taliesin*:

> The Taliesin and Gwion Bach tales are translated from the late seventeenth-century manuscript National

Library of Wales MS.6209E, copied by David Parry (an amanuensis of Edward Lhuyd) from the sixteenth-century text of Elis Gruffydd . . . Lady Guest did not have access to this manuscript; her translation of the tale, which differs substantially from the one offered here, was based on eighteenth-century Welsh manuscript sources.

In other words, his source, he considers, is the more authentic. Certainly it has the benefit of being free of any taint of the hand of Iolo Morganwg. We thus have to take seriously the possibility that the story of the weir originated in Conwy Bay and was transferred to Aberdyfi, perhaps by Iolo Morganwg himself. Interestingly a tradition seems to have survived locally that Gwyddno's Weir, which Elffin fished, was in Conwy Bay: Llandudno's earliest guidebook, published in 1849, says that Gwyddno 'resided also for some time in the neighbourhood. The latter had near his residence a weir, called Gored Wyddno (*Gwyddno's Weir*), which is even yet known by the same name, and belongs to the Hon. Mr Mostyn, as owner of the house of Bodscallan'. We shall be visiting this theme again in a later chapter.

This location of the Cantref Gwaelod events in Conwy Bay, if we accepted it, would be a complete reversal of the normal view, as for instance put forward by North, that the Conwy Bay story of Helig was a mere borrowing of the Cardigan Bay story of Gwyddno. North says, for instance, dismissively:

The thesis that the story of Helig is not history has been supplemented by the suggestion that it is not even genuine local folk-lore, but is a legend brought from another area and made to relate to Conway Bay.

There is no mention at this stage, however, of any inundation. It is only later that it comes to be assumed that Elffin is fishing the weir because that is all that is left of his father's drowned lands; and that his misfortune in losing his inheritance is supposed to be compensated by what he finds – eventually the poet-prophet Taliesin – in the weir. In that version he comes to visit his uncle, Maelgwn, at Deganwy, rather than starting from there, the Aberdyfi location of his weir being by then thoroughly established.

It was Thomas Love Peacock who set out for us the full story of Gwyddno, Seithenyn, Elphin and Taliesin, in his early novel *The Misfortunes of Elphin*. Peacock used his wide knowledge of Welsh tradition to invent his own version of the tale, in doing so continuing a quite respectable tradition which has from time to time caused step-changes in our knowledge of our own lore. Geoffrey of Monmouth, and indeed to some extent Iolo Morganwg, were not in their own eyes the charlatans which modern scholarship might like to portray them as being. Similarly Peacock was no mere fanciful entertainer. He was using authentic matter – the story of Taliesin, as it was available to him – for a new purpose.

The Misfortunes of Elphin, Peacock's fifth novel, published in 1829, may be seen as a romantic dalliance with the idea of Welshness, or alternatively, as it is more often, as a political satire – a tamer type of Swift's *Gulliver* – which used sixth century Wales as a cover. Peacock, essentially a Londoner, had good reason to feel romantic about North Wales. In 1810 to 1811 he spent some months there, and there he met his future wife, Jane Gryffyth. In 1812 he was introduced to Shelley, who moved in that year to Tremadog. That was the year that Madock's great embankment being built across the estuary of the Glaslyn burst, flooding his recently reclaimed land. Peacock cannot have been unaware of this catastrophe, and it can hardly have been out of his head when he describes, in *Elphin*, the breaking of the embankment of Elphin's kingdom which the drunken Seithenyn allowed to fall into disrepair; and the flooding of the fertile land. We know that he saw Madock's embankment finally repaired, in 1815, since he described the effect of it in changing the landscape in his novel *Headlong Hall*, published in 1816:

> The mountain frame remains unchanged, unchangeable; but the liquid mirror it enclosed is gone.

An ironic reversal of the view attributed to the survivors of Elffin's, or Helig's, flood, in which the liquid mirror covers the once-hospitable ground.

Peacock's location, following the Triads and the manuscript used by Lady Charlotte (which had already been published in part by Dr Owen Pughe in the Cambrian Quarterly), was given some support by the existence (with traditions surrounding them) of an offshore outcrop of stone: the remarkable straight bank of Sarn Badrig, which runs for thirteen to fourteen miles out to sea from a mile offshore from the coast between Harlech and Barmouth, and so may well be thought to have been Seithenyn's embankment, once it is decided that the site of his court is supposed to be located here.

IV Irrecoverable as Lyonesse

Here is an old guidebook, *Nooks and Corners of Cornwall*, opening the chapter headed THE LAND OF LYONESSE:

> If you ask the people they will tell you that without doubt the piece of water between the south of Cornwall and the Scillies was once dry land . . . The fishermen, looking down through the clear waters on a still day, declare they can make out the ruins of old churches and houses, and that their nets have brought them time and again articles of household economy, pieces of broken doors and roofs and windows.

What happened, it goes on to say, was that the sea broke in upon the land, and one man, whose name was Trevelyan, leapt on his white horse and rode ahead of the waves to take refuge in a cave in Cornwall, from where, looking back when the storm had passed, he saw only 'a wide stretch of waters, with the Scillies sparkling in the distance'.

Here then, in confident balance, are the two elements: a posited historical record evidenced by present-day phenomena, and a fanciful heroic tale. Both, in this example, are undated, though the guidebook makes a reference to the 'Saxon Chronicle' as saying that 'the sea broke in upon the land and swallowed up many towns and a countless multitude of people', though not specifying where. The passage actually comes from the entry in *The Anglo-Saxon*

Chronicles for the year 1014, which largely deals with the confrontation of Aethelred and Cnut in Lincolnshire and Kent. It reads (in Anne Savage's translation): 'This year on Michaelmas Eve came the great sea-flood widely through this land, and it ran up farther than it ever had, flooded many towns, and drowned countless human beings.' The supposed finding in fishing-nets of household items and materials would infer an inundation even later than that, and may, if it occurred, have another explanation.

In any case both purported fact and emotive fable have a common interest: the lost land; and perhaps it is in the poignancy of this that the fascination of all our flood stories lies. It is the image itself of the lostness of the past. 'Oxford' (writes Evelyn Waugh in *Brideshead Revisited*) '– submerged now and obliterated, irrecoverable as Lyoness, so quickly have the waters come flooding in – Oxford, in those days, was still a city of aquatint'.

In the first volume of *Antiquity*, of March 1927, the first article is called simply 'Lyonesse', by O.G.S. Crawford, who also happened to be the journal's editor.

Crawford, then aged forty-one, was at the time an archaeology officer with the Ordnance Survey.

Once upon a time (so tradition says) a region of extreme fertility lay between the Scilly Islands and Cornwall. This land was called Lyonesse; and where now roll the waters of the Atlantic there once stood prosperous towns and no less than a hundred and forty churches.

Crawford seeks to answer the question whether this 'famous legend' has 'any real basis in fact'. He cites the Rev. William Borlase, writing in 1753, as an early source for the evidence

47

that the islands were once joined up: The 'flats' are 'quite dry at a spring tide, and men may easily pass dry-shod from one island to another . . . ' Walls and ruins, Borlase says, are frequently discovered among the sandbanks.

The year before, Crawford had been to see for himself. On the day of the lowest of the spring tides (March 16th) he hired a boat, and investigated the straight line of stones on the beach below the uninhabited island of Samson. He found that they were indeed the remains of a wall. 'It was one of those thrilling moments which occasionally occur in the life of an archaeologist. Here before us was tangible proof that the land had sunk since prehistoric times; for no one makes walls like this below high water mark.' His reason for assuming the prehistoric nature of the work rested, it seems, on comparison with prehistoric walls elsewhere on the islands. Yet he himself says that walls are made there in exactly the same way today, so this carries no weight.

It is easy to show, and Crawford does, that a lowering of the sea by 60 feet, which would make the underwater field-walls functional, would turn the Scilly Isles into one large island. The most habitable and fertile parts of this were of course the bits which were drowned.

This is not quite the same as saying that the Scillies were once joined to Cornwall, and it says nothing either about the date. There is indeed evidence that in the 3rd and 4th centuries A.D. the area was an island, and only one: Solinus, writing in about 240, calls it 'Siluram insulam', and Sulpicius Severus, writing about 400 A.D. of events which took place in the time of Maximus, in 387, refers to 'Sylina Insula'.

Crawford then seems to be saying that the Lyonesse story is far from being fable. The fishermen in my *Nooks and Corners* book were not as merely legendary as they sounded. They spoke to Crawford too, in 1926, and not of some half-

The hill still known as Trwyn yr Wylfa is supposed in the legend to be the place from which the survivors looked back at the drowned land.

The rediscovered MS of the 'Notes to be Observed' shows changes clearly made by the author. The hand is not that of Sir John Wynn.

INTERESTING DISCOVERY IN CONWAY BAY.

TREE TRUNKS IN THE NORTH CHANNEL.

Another discovery of great interest has been made by Mr John Roberts, Bryn Celyn, who, our readers will be glad to learn, will resulme his articles on "Llandudno as it Was" in our next issue. Mr Roberts has devoted considerable time to the examination of the sands, both in Llandudno and Conway bays, and was rewarded recently by a discovery, concerning which he writes as follows:—

"On August 2nd I went for a stroll on the Conway Shore, the tide that day being a low spring one. Years ago the North Channel, used by ships to enter Conway harbour, was about half-a-mile out from high water mark, but recently it has moved, and is now quite close to the shore. Thousands of tons of sand appear to have been carried away and the bottom of the channel has been laid bare. It has not been in this state within the memory of anyone now living, probably centuries have passed since it bore a similar appearance.

"In this channel, which is situated about 200 yards to the s.w. from the Toll House, I found the remains of trees embedded in the hard red clay. There were four stumps projecting out, and are undoubtedly in the position in which they grew. I traced one root and found that it was about 20 feet long and from 8 inches to 3 inches in diameter.

"A short distance to the N.W. I found another stump with roots extending about seven feet long. Turning to the S.E. I came across another trunk—an enormous one—and roots. The roots were, I should say, from 18 inches to 2 feet in diameter. Near the end of the protecting wall on the beach, about two yards from high water mark, I found what appeared to be the remains of a gigantic tree.

"It would be very interesting if the materials about the tree were excavated in order that it may be properly examined. Does not this go a long way to prove that what is now Conway Bay was at one time inhabited land?"

We understand that Mr Roberts intends making further investigations when the tide permits, the results of which will be published in our columns.

INVALID SHELTERS.—The Surveyor presented plans and estimates at a meeting of the Llandudno Works Committee of the two Invalid Shelters for forwarding to the Local Government Board in applying for a loan of £371, to defray the cost of the work. Plans and estimate

Llandudno Advertiser, 25 Sept, 1909

Many examples of submerged forests can still be clearly seen around our coast at low tide.

Firmly rooted in clay, and still wooden in texture, examples of these have been dated to nearly 7,000 years before present.

mences a week's engagement on Monday evening, and may be relied upon to provide us with real vocal treats nightly during her stay.

* * *

THE AUTUMN SERIES.

On October 11th the Autumn Series of concerts will commence. The same orchestra, which is now giving such a good account of itself is being retained, and the Committee have arranged for additional items to the ordinary programme, including Mr Leslie Harris, the society entertainer. Mr Harris requires no introduction to Llandudnoites, and we should think there are few if any visitors who have not heard of him. He is quite the most popular and gifted entertainers on the concert platform in England to-day and will undoubtedly draw big attendances. Mr Coleman, baritone, Miss Marion Beeley, contralto; Miss Johnson, contralto; Mr John Booth, tenor, and Miss Lucy Nuttall, contralto, are amongst the other artistes engaged during the three weeks' series. During the third week Mr Harry Liston and party will give matinees daily, and on Thursday, October 21st, the Carnarvon Choral Society, winners at this year's National Eisteddfod, and numbering 180 voices, have been retained to provide a specially attractive programme.

THE SUBMERGED FOREST IN CONWAY BAY.

On Thursday evening a small party consisting of Mr John Roberts, Bryn Celyn; Mr W. R. Brookes, Mr F. Holland, Mr Williams, woodwork instructor at the County School, and Mr A. R. Hughes visited the Conway Shore to further examine the remains of trees lately discovered by Mr Roberts in the bed of the North Channel. The tide was very low and the conditions favourable for careful examination.

The first tree to be visited was the very large one that lies within a few yards of high water mark, where the sea wall commences below the Gogarth Abbey Hotel. This was quickly located, and Mr W. Owen, beach inspector, coming on the scene produced a spade, with the aid of which portions of it were laid bare, showing it to be the remains of what must have been at one time a gigantic oak. The roots were very hard, but portions were chipped off and carried away as curios. In connection with this particular tree, Mr Owen said its existence had been known for some time, and that in the old days fishermen used to cut off pieces of it to make netting needles, the hardness of the wood rendering it an ideal material for that purpose.

From this tree a descent was made to the channel proper, Mr Roberts leading the way. But a very short distance had to be covered before the party got to the blue clay which forms the bottom of the channel. This being entirely denuded of sand made the task of locating the remains of the trees an easy one, for the stumps of more than one protruded above the clay. Chunks were broken off and

subsoil. I am writing this to you to try and call the attention of your local authorities to this very interesting discovery on the foreshore of this beautiful town.

Interesting, not only as a delightful holiday resort, but also for its geological and pantological records, which may if collected throw a glare of light on the great problems of the newly-budding evolutionary history of our wonderful world.

Mounting to the summit of the Great Orme we find one great mound already opened out by quarrying, plainly revealing its internal structure as a concretion of limestone fossils; mostly oyster shells of arctic and probably of extinct species. Thus showing that the Orme must have been deeply submerged when the living creatures of the sea built us this massive knoll.

It is most likely this took place during one of the inter-glacial depressions that, according to such well-informed geologists as Professor Ramsey, slowly intervened during those long and silent ages of the remote past, and of which North Wales can show so many records. Even the sand hills, fringing the West Shore, are now found to be really sand-covered glacial moraines, left there by a glacier that slowly ploughed its way down the Conway Valley, after grinding and leaving its marks at the corner of the valley of Bettws, rounding the hard rocks at a point near Pont-y-Pair and finally depositing a part of its accumulated store of tell-tale polished, and striated boulders to enrich the western shore of Llandudno. One of the most finished and beautiful glacial boulders still projects out there at the corner of the moraine section pointing along the line of "black rocks" left at a long trail, plainly indicating the slow weathering back of the sea coast.

Professor Ramsey, who for many years held the position of chief of the Geological Survey of North Wales, says that the whole rock surface of the island of Anglesea has been polished and striated, during this same glacial period, by a great glacier that ploughed its way down from the hills of Cumberland, and through thousands of years of continuous work, managed to scoop out the valley of the Straits, and so made Anglesea into an island.

And now comes Mr Roberts, who from the days of his boyhood, has been searching out the hidden mysteries of this wonderful coast. And his discoveries plainly show that the Great Orme has at one time been much higher above the surface of the sea as well as alternately below the surface.

And now, surely such wonderful and far-reaching discoveries should appeal to the enthusiasm of the local authorities to do something to unearth and fully determine the full meaning of such discoveries as these, indicating as most probably they do, a long lost and submerged forest of pines.—Yours truly,

J. R. DAVISON (Crewe).

Bod Gwilym,
Vaughan Street, Llandudno.

Llandudno Advertiser, 2 October, 1909.

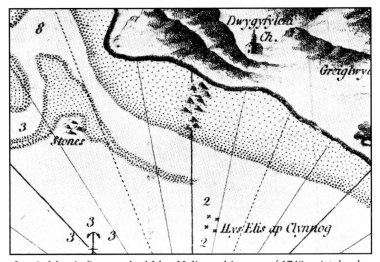

Lewis Morris first marked Llys Helig on his map of 1748, mistakenly calling it Llys Ellis ap Clynnog: an error still copied from his on admiralty charts today.

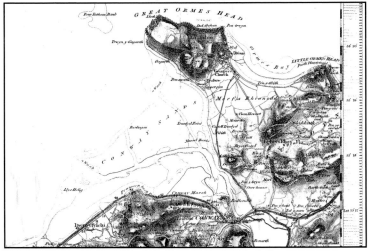

The first edition of the Ordnance Survey map for our area in 1841, marks the Llys Helig reef, but a little too far north.

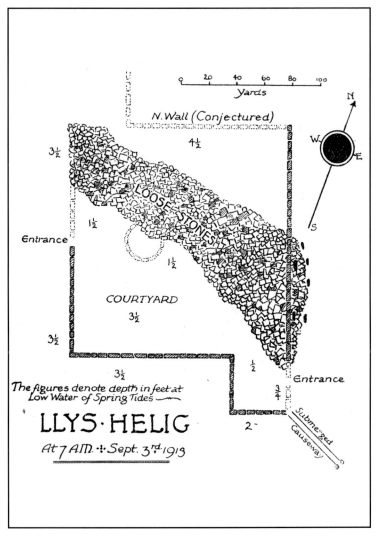

The figures denote depth in feet at Low Water of Spring Tides

LLYS·HELIG

At 7 A.M. ‡ Sept. 3rd 1913

The trip by Horace Lees in 1913 confirmed Ashton's impression in 1908, that there is evidence of 'straight lines' and 'right-angles in the southern part of the site.

THE SUPPOSED SUBMERGED PALACE.

LLYS HELYG EXPLORATION PARTY.

On Wednesday afternoon of this week a number of members of the Llandudno Field Club made an attempt to inspect the ruins of the palace of Helig ap Glanwg, Lord of Cantraf Gwaelod, which are believed to be situate between Llandudno and Penmaenmawr, in the estuary of the River Conway, about two miles from Penmaenmawr. Several previous expeditions for the same purpose have been made at various times, but since Mr Bezant Lowe and Mr W. J. P. Arrowsmith, of Deganwy, in September 1907, visited the site, and the inspection of Mr William Ashton last September, there has been a growing feeling locally that a further attempt should be made to explore the site of the palace, and if possible, obtain drawings or photographs of the stones. The present equinoctial tides are calculated to be the highest that have occurred for the past 22 years, and at midday on Tuesday the highest of these tides was expected. The higher the tide, the lower the succeeding ebb, and it was therefore expected that an exceptionally good opportunity would be afforded of

in the chain of evidence relating to the legend of Llys Helig was laid bare. It had been recognised by this time that whatever the groups of boulders might be they were not part of the palace itself, but there was some reason for surmising that they might have either formed part of an ancient wall surrounded the palace, or even of the causeway alleged to have been in existence at that time. The very low ebb gave the excavators every opportunity, and a few minutes' vigorous work exposed what looked very like a wall. The stones even to a layman bore every appearance of having been placed together by human agency, and the expressed opinions of experts on such building matters as Mr Humphreys and Mr John Roberts confirmed the impression. It should also be stated that the conjectured exposed wall ran in a line for the shore bearing in the direction of Penmaenbach. Samples of the stones and the packing between the stones were dug out and taken for further investigation. In addition to this many examples of flat-faced stones roughly-squared were noted continuing in the same direction and also scattered over a little wider area. Photographs of the part were taken, but the light, never very good, was failing rapidly, so they may not come out very clearly. Certainly geologists may demolish the theory, but

pieces like dry clay when layered with a small steel bar, or when kicked. The stumps of the trees with the roots spreading therefrom, were clearly defined, the roots being specially clear; in fact, they looked just like the decayed stumps and roots seen in the ordinary wood where bared of the surface soil. The grain of the wood was most clearly seen in the trunks and the roots. One straight root measured 20ft. long from the tree trunk to where it dipped and was lost in the clay, and it was about 12in. diameter at the trunk end and about 4in. diameter at the other end. Other roots measured up to 12ft. long and varied from the thickness of a man's thigh to about 1in. diameter.

The exception previously referred to was a tree stump standing up about 12 inches above the red clay. It was not one of the largest trees though it was the only really hard one. The heart of the trunk was fairly sound and only with considerable difficulty could it be cut with a knife. We broke three small pieces from this trunk with the steel bar, Mr Roberts taking one piece, and I have the other two, together with a chipping cut off with a knife. These samples show that the trees were oak trees.

In laying down the bearings on a map, I find the centre of the red clay patch

Llandudno Advertiser, 27 March, 1909.

LLYS HELIG MYSTERY UNSOLVED

STONES NOT PALACE RUINS SAY EXPERTS

NEW THEORIES FOLLOW DAWN EXPEDITION

The veracity of the captivating legend of Llys Helig (Helig's Palace), and the "great inundation," which resulted in both the palace and acres of fertile land becoming part of the Irish sea bed, received a severe blow when, shortly

The North Wales Weekly News, 1939.

The early photographs reproduced in Asthon's book show apparent
lines of stone, including a zig-zag shape to the south.

F.J. North was of the opinion that the apparently straight lines and regular angles of the stones were a result of lines of vision.

North's photographs show that much of the site consists of shapeless banks of stone.

North's view of Deganwy was that an with an apparently straight band of boulders resulted from the denudation of the clay; the alignment is not the result of human intervention.

North also thought that a similar stretch of boulders and pebbles resulted from the denudation of boulder clay, and reproduced the floor conditions that obtain in the central part of the Llys Helig site.

Llys Helig Story

"FULL OF INACCURACIES"

Expert Examination

The picturesque legend of the great inundation of the lands of Prince Helig and the subsequent belief that peculiar rock - formations entirely submerged in Conway Bay, about a mile and a half from Penmaenmawr, except during exceptionally low tides, were the remains of Helig's "palace," have been unconditionally discredited by two leading scientists—Dr. F. J. North, geologist of the National Museum of Wales, and Mr. W. F. Grimes, of the Office of Works (Ordnance Survey department).

On Thursday evening, at the Llandudno Public Library, members of the Llandudno and Colwyn Bay Field Club heard Dr. North literally put "finis" to the legend. Dr. North and Mr. Grimes (the latter in a report which was read in his absence by the chairman, Dr. Willoughby Gardner) declare emphatically that there was not a shred of evidence to prove that the weed-covered rocks which were inspected by the expedition on August 17 last could have been the remains of any kind of building.

Recounting the legend of Prince Helig and the great inundation which, according to the oft-repeated tradition, submerged his palace and rich lands in the fifth or sixth century, Dr. Willoughby Gardner said this was so widely believed that nearly all old families in Wales took delight in contending they could trace back their ancestry to Helig, whom they regarded as a hero. After speaking of previous expeditions to the reputed site of the "palace," Dr. Gardner suggested that some previous findings had apparently tended to corroborate the legend and the belief that the submerged rocks were the relics of an ancient building. But there had always been a controversy, and it was with the view of settling the matter for all time that the assistance of Dr. North and Mr. Grimes was sought and the expedition of August 17 arranged.

"COLLECTION OF STONES."

Mr. Grimes, in his written report, stated he was dealing with the matter solely from an archaeological viewpoint.

"What I saw with my eyes, and felt with my hands and feet (Mr. Grimes, wearing a bathing costume, walked on the rocks) has made me decide that this collection of stones is not the remains of any ancient palace or any other kind of structure. They have ceased, in so far as I am concerned, to have any archaeological significance."

The stones showed no signs of having formed the walls of any kind of dwelling. He also pointed out that large stones were to be found at the top, together with small ones. Even ordinary field boundary walls had the larger stones at the bottom. While he could not account for the peculiar alignment of the stones, he insisted that below water they extended over a wide area, giving him the impression of being just an unbroken mass of boulders massed high at some points as compared with others. He thought excavation of the site, even if that were possible, would corroborate his views.

Dr. North prefaced his remarks by stating that his interest in the legend dated back to 1913 when he heard of the various previous expeditions to the site and the belief that it represented the lost palace of Prince Helig. But although a student then, he soon formed the opinion that the amount of submergence which would have been necessary to permit the inundation was contrary to all reckonings and known facts, and therefore the belief that the rocks represented the site of the fifth century palace was unfounded. He expressed his views on the matter at a lecture and was strongly criticised, and, possibly, it had been hoped that the August 17 expedition would have resulted in his having to eat his own words. He had no intention of concurring with such a desire. Recalling the discussions which immediately followed the completion of the expedition, Dr. North said he determined to trace back the legend, if possible, to its very beginning, and, in consequence, had read 115 books and manuscripts as well as sixty letters dealing with it.

SIR JOHN WYNN STARTED THE HARE.

The "villain of the piece," he said, was the little book "An Ancient Survey of Penmaenmawr," by Sir John Wynn of Gwydir (1553-1626). The book was split into three parts, which were completely unrelated one to the other and were copies of manuscripts which had probably belonged to Sir John Wynn and which were found after his death and copied a hundred years later. The portion dealing with the Helig family was full of inaccuracies.

"Referring to one of the many "inaccuracies," Dr. North said: "You will find in tracing Helig's ancestry that some people come in at awkward times. His grandfather was alive in 807, but according to other facts Helig himself died in the sixth century. The same applies to the person stated to be his great-grandmother; she was not born when Helig died."

He contended that there was more imagination than history in the legend, and added that he had looked everywhere for some slight confirmation of the story.

Referring to the early chronicles written by various writers and dealing with happenings during the supposed Helig period, he pointed out that, while mention was made of minor floods in those chronicles, no mention was made of any great submergence and inundation which, according to the legend destroyed Helig's property. "This would have been a major event and had it happened would have undoubtedly been recorded by those early writers," he added.

Putting the legend out of his mind, he had tried to find if there ever was a Prince Helig. He discovered the name Helig mentioned six times during different periods, but never was there coupled with the name of any of the six Heligs of one of the same losing all by the submergence of his lands. No book mentioned the legend and probably no credence was given to it until Sir John Wynn expressed his beliefs, which were further embellished by subsequent writers, one of whom, a rector of Denbigh, went so far as to state that the "disaster was foretold many years before it happened in the 800's." The discrepancy of 300 years or so apparently did not matter!

"NEITHER GOOD LEGEND NOR GENUINE FOLK-LORE."

The story was neither good legend nor genuine folk-lore, said Dr. North, and went on to state that similar stories were current in Cardigan Bay, Ireland and Brittany.

By means of explanatory lantern slides, Dr. North showed that the submergence of the Welsh coast took place thousands of years before the stated date of Helig's existence. Further slides showed how the rocks at the site were identical with those known to have been brought to the sea during the ice age, and how their peculiar wall-like formation could be compared with similar boulders which form the

Marcus Elliott on the northern reef.

A shapeless scattering of stones is all that is revealed over much of the visible site.

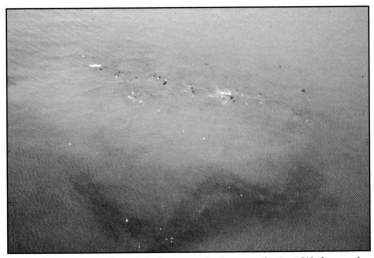

Nigel Bannerman's aerial photograph shows a distinct W shape of rocks lying under water in the southern sector of the site.

'Gorad Wyddno' off the 'Black Rocks' between Deganwy and Llandudno, when viewed at a certain level of tide, shows a distinct V shape very similar to the lines and right-angles photographed at Llys Helig..

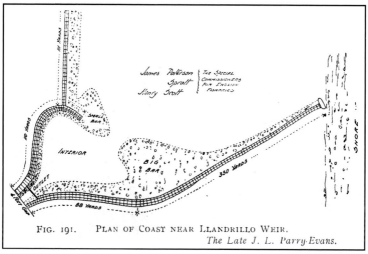

FIG. 191.   PLAN OF COAST NEAR LLANDRILLO WEIR.
The Late J. L. Parry-Evans.

'Gorad Faelgwn', lying alongside 'Gorad Wyddno', has a more curved line, but is recognisably formed.

The fish-weir at Rhos Fynach survived into the 20th century, and shows the characteristic structure of boulders shaped into a V, topped by stables and wattles.

A plan of the Rhos weir sows angles and curved as well as straight lines in the construction of the funnel state.

The Bishop's Palace on the Great Orme is now largely collapsed into the sea.

remembered prehistoric past, but of features visible to him, and more so to them (' . . .they still observe them, and told me of the existence of others that I have not yet been able to go and see'). It is no surprise, of course that it is always fishermen, in the stories, who report these sightings, whether on lakes or in coastal waters. We see the surface and the reflected image; they are the ones concerned with what lies beneath it, the sandbanks which restrict their passage, and the outcrops which snare their nets.

The country of Lyonesse (in the form 'Lyones') first occurs in our written tradition in Sir Thomas Malory's Arthurian material, one book of which is called 'Sir Tristram de Lyones'. 'There was a kynge,' it begins, 'that hyght Melyodas, and he was lorde of the contrey of Lyones.' Sir Tristram inherits. Introducing himself he says: 'Sir, my name is Trystram, and in the contrey of Lyonesse was I borne.'

Malory was writing in the late 1460's, working from earlier French material. His Tristram book has as its main source the French Prose Romance of Tristran, dating from about 1230, where the country of Leonois is clearly assumed (as it is in Malory) to lie adjacent to Cornwall.

Malory does not say explicitly that Lyonesse was actually joined to Cornwall, but this is certainly implied. He does not refer to it as an island. Indeed it seems to be much more than that. King Meliodas goes hunting in a forest big enough for him to be lost in, and his wife, searching for him, goes 'far in the forest', where she gives birth to Tristram. He too when he grows up does much hunting and hawking. The characters in the story travel by sea to and from Brittany and Ireland; but Tristram at one point rides, apparently from Lyoness, into Cornwall.

It is odd that the French book associates Lyonesse with Cornwall, since its name connects it to the southern French town of Lyon, which the Romans founded in 43 A.D. as Lugdunum. When 'Lugdunensem' occurs in the work of the Roman historian of the fourth century A.D., Ammianus Marcellinus, it is translated in the standard English text as 'Lyonesse': 'The first Lyonesse province is made famous by Lyons . . . ' The name Lugdunum connects the place with the god whom the Celts worshipped in Gaul by the name Lugus, the Irish god Lugh, who reappears in Welsh tradition as Lleu Llaw Gyffes and possibly later as Sir Lancelot du Lac. Besides Lyons he gave his name to Laon, to the town of Leiden in Holland and to Carlisle in Britain. It is his death in August that is commemorated by the Irish festival of Lugnasad, or Lammas. The Romans equated Lugus with Mercury, and Julius Caesar, who made a first-hand study of Druidism in Gaul, even getting to know a druid personally, tells us 'The god they reverence most is Mercury. They have very many images of him, and regard him as the inventor of all arts . . . ' It would not be surprising then, given the great importance of this deity, if there were more than one Lugdunensem, or Lyonesse.

In his article in *Antiquity* Crawford cites submerged forests as evidence of changes in sea-level, and also mentions the case of a stone circle in Brittany (on the island of Er Lanic) which is now half under water. Since Malory's Tristram also had dealings with Brittany it seems natural to follow these leads. Perhaps we should go there next.

What Crawford does not say, though he might well have, is that Brittany has its own inundation legend, and that this is remarkably similar (with a slight difference of emphasis) to those of Llys Helig, Cantre'r Gwaelod, and Lyonesse.

Although the earliest reference to the legend of Ker Is is in Pierre Le Baud's *Histoire de Bretagne* of the start of the 16th century, the fullest and most influential version is probably to be found in a poem by Hersart de la Villemarqué of 1845. King Grallon of Cornouaille (now a region of south-west Brittany, but in the Middle Ages a more extensive kingdom, with Quimper as its capital) was rebuked by a saint for dissipation. It may have been as retribution for this that he was betrayed by his daughter. She, incited by her lover, stole the keys to the sea-defences and drowned the city. The king and daughter escaped the flood on horseback, but he wisely cast her off en route, and came safely to land. Since Villemarqué was both a modifier of traditional ballads and a scholar of Welsh and Breton literature, we need not be surprised to find an echo of the early Welsh poem which includes the apparently guilty girl and a horseride.

'Ker Is' means lowest fortress, Caer Isaf in Welsh, and so much the same as Cantre'r Gwaelod, *(lowest hundred)*. It is traditionally set in the Bay of Douarnenez, off the north coast of the Cornouaille peninsula, but 17th century accounts of a road from Quimper to submerged buildings in the Baie des Trespassés, lying between the Pointe du Raz and the Pointe du Van on Cape Sizun, the peninsula's most western point, provide a possible rival. Local legend places the town of 'Is' in a marshy valley in the bay. On the other hand equivalent legends were current by the 17th century on the shores of the Bay of Douarnenez, where, moreover, Breton tradition sites the palace of King Mark, whose nephew Tristan gave his name to the island at the mouth of the Pouldavid estuary. Finds, report the guidebooks, have been uncovered in both bays and also off the Penmarch Peninsula, Cornouaille's southern tip.

King Grallon, or in some accounts Gradlon, was moved by his adventure to take up a life of virtue, and a statue of him stands between the two towers of the cathedral of Quimper, which town he chose for his new capital. His daughter, cast into the sea, became a mermaid, known as Marie-Morgane, and still lures sailors to their fate. The remedy (if one is to believe the Michelin guide) is to hold a Good Friday mass in one of the churches of the drowned city.

The wickedness, it seems, has been transferred in the Breton version from the king to the daughter, and the whole thing set in an ecclesiastical context. Here saints do the warning less explicitly conferred in the British versions. In fact the seminal source is perhaps Albert le Grand's *Vies des Saints de la Bretaigne Armorique* of 1637, where the shameless daughter first makes her appearance in the 1680 edition.

The Breton legends claim to concern the 6th century A.D., as do the British ones; but we have considered the unlikelihood of this being historical, since other records would exist for that time. Rachel Bromwich, a Celtic scholar, whose article 'Cantre'r Gwaelod and Ker Is' appeared in *The Early Cultures of North-West Europe*, edited by Cyril Fox and Bruce Dickens, in 1950, comes to much the same conclusion as North in *Sunken Cities* five years later (though he does not seem to have known of her work).

> . . . geological evidence will not countenance the possibility of any substantial marine transgression at a period more recent than the Bronze Age. Moreover, if several such spectacular inundations had taken place within historical times, one might expect that some allusion to at least one such event might have been preserved by Latin authorities.

Clearly the sites we have visited so far in this chapter have something in common with each other, and with the Welsh ones which are our main concern. These places are all part of the Celtic fringe. Hence it is not surprising that they share the same stories. They are all coastal and settled places, so we might expect erosion by the sea, if it took place, to have affected them in similar ways. It is North who points to another common factor: they are all on an ancient sea-route.

> . . . it cannot be altogether without significance that the route by which the megalithic cultures reached Britain from the Mediterranean lay past Brittany and the Scilly Isles on its way to the channel between Wales and Ireland.

Of course the first part of this is not strictly true: it could perfectly well be altogether without significance. It is true, however, that the similarities of structure in tomb-building links western Britain with the Mediterranean area, while the differences of the development of its style indicates a temporal process underlying this link. Glyn Daniel, in his book *The Megalith Builders of Western Europe* finds that the distinctive chamber tomb form of burial arose in the eastern Mediterranean in the 3rd millennium B.C. (in Minoan and Mycenean cultures). It is from there that it eventually came to us. 'We do now have good archaeological evidence of contacts between the Mycenean world and the Early Bronze Age people of southern Britain . . . ' If then the Mediterranean examples are older, the route to Britain inevitably came past here, past Brittany and the Scillies. This is not to say that there is any reason to suppose the flood-myth came with the tomb-builders, or rather with their influence (since we do not need to suppose that they, as distinct from their culture, actually moved). Trade routes are important in the two-way dissemination of ideas and innovations, influences spreading through local communities like a flooding tide.

There is, though, evidence from the Latin sources themselves, that peoples with inundations in their history and a folk tradition of displacement came as well from the other direction. The late Roman historian Ammianus Marcellinus was writing, in the second half of the 4th century A.D., about the people of Gaul during the first century B.C., when the Romans came there. His source, he says, was the Alexandrian Greek historian Timagenes, who wrote, from earlier records already lost, during the first century A.D. Of the origins of the Gauls, also known as the Celts, his *Res Gestae*, XV., 9, has the following remarkable passage.

3. Some asserted that the people first seen in these regions were Aborigines, called Celts from the name of a beloved king . . . Others stated that the Dorians, following the earlier Hercules, settled in the lands bordering on the Ocean. 4. The Druids say that a part of the people was in fact indigenous, but that others also poured in from remote islands and the regions across the Rhine, driven from their homes by continual wars and by the inundation of the stormy sea.

' . . . alluvione fervidi maris sedibus suis expulsos.' This is not, as one might have expected, the record of a mystical or symbolic folk-wisdom, but a report of what the Druids evidently took to be hard historic fact: namely that at some distant time there occurred a rising of the sea level along the coast of the Low Countries – the 'tractibus transhenanis', the river Rhine separating Gaul from what is now the Netherlands – an incursion sufficient to cause the displacement of large numbers of people. Meic Stephens, in his *Oxford Companion to the Literature of Wales*, says that the best known version of the Cantre'r Gwaelod story 'is about three hundred years old and derives from similar stories in the Low Countries', but without unfortunately specifying these. It would of course be odd if places such as Holland (famous for the boy who blocked a hole in a dyke with his finger, and so saved the land from flood) did not at one time have their own body of inundation legends, which do not however appear to have been preserved.

Given the Druids' well-attested role of preserving and transmitting an established canon of oral tradition, the occurrence Ammianus Marcellinus reports them as recording might have taken place a thousand or more years before their time. It is not clear from the classical authors whether their people's history was a part of their teachings, but from the above quotation it seems that people referred to them for this knowledge, and Caesar clearly confirms this when he says of the Gauls that they 'claim all to be descended from Father Dis, declaring that this is the tradition preserved by the Druids'.

In view of these testimonies we have to take the Druids seriously on this issue, if, as seems highly likely, they are correctly reported by Ammianus Marcellinus.

Crawford, who seems to have had a particular interest in the matter, pulls us back from prehistory and coastal erosion into more explicitly local legends, in (as he says) the heart of England. He says at the end of his article that of the Shropshire meres 'many folk tales are told, recalling times when the site was occupied by a palace, town, or church; and it is said that the bells of the church still lie there, and have even been seen and heard'. These remarks caused a correspondence to start with a lady named Lily Chitty, an expert on the Shropshire meres, who intended to write an article for *Antiquity*, which Crawford hoped to publish. This apparently never took place, but the hand-written notes are available in the County archives in Shrewsbury's Records and Research Centre, from which it emerges that you can hear the bells ringing if you go out to the middle of Marton Pool on Christmas Eve, that towers and chimneys may be seen under the waters of Llyn Llynclys, near Oswestry, where, remarkably, at the dissolute court before the inundation 'on feast days an unearthly voice was heard, "Daw dial, daw!" (*"Vengeance will come, will come!"*)'. And when? In the sixth generation, according to Ms Chitty's notes. A family gathering; a feast; the harpist goes out to take the night air, turns back and finds it all gone. 'In its place the rippling surface of a lake'. It is of course not all that far for these themes to have migrated from Bala to Oswestry, but puzzling as to why the details should be so often precisely the same.

Lily Chitty gives evidence of dug-out canoes and submerged causeways (as at Ellesmere) for the ancient existence of lake-dwellings and their destruction by rising water. The underwater causeway at Ellesmere appears to be well-attested. Divers found it when looking for someone who had drowned, in September 1879.

Crawford, who probably didn't know about Chitty when he wrote his article, gives as his reference Charlotte Burne's *Shropshire Folklore*, in which we find a similar story of wickedness punished by inundation at Bomere, and ringing bells at Croesmere and Colemere.

Everybody seems to be able to point to a parallel case, and Thomas Pennant, writing in 1778 in his *Tours in Wales* (in which he relates Cantre'r Gwaelod firmly to the causeway Sarn Badrig, and says that it was 'overwhelmed by the sea, about the year 500') is reminded of a case he came across in Essex:

> A similar accident happened in some distant period on the coast of Essex. The canons of *St Paul* must be possessed of a prebend, before they can become residentiaries; and the one usually given is, *The praebenda consumpta per mare*, which lay on the coast of that country.

This on the face of it could hardly be more obscure and forms an example of the often bizarre ramifications of any historical investigation. The place in question is Walton on the Naze, and the only known reference to the story is in volume 2 of the Reverend Philip Morant's *The History and Antiquities of the County of Essex*, first published in 1763, and so available to Pennant:

> Here was formerly the endowment, or corps, of one of the Prebends of St Paul's, London; but the sea hath consumed or devoured it long ago. Therefore it is styled Praebenda Consumpta per mare. It has the thirteenth stall on the left side of the choir; and is valued at 1 mark.

If nothing else, this should usefully remind us that we must not become tempted to think of loss of land to the sea as being tied to some period in remote prehistory, since St Paul's, perhaps in the Middle Ages, lost a mark's revenue to it and inscribed the record on a choir stall.

Once again, in this chapter, we have seen a strange ambiguity between fact and fable, with one lot of experts wanting to show how the story, as folk tradition, might have spread in prehistoric times along the western seaboard of northern Europe, and another group demonstrating with equal clarity how the stories could have arisen locally in later times from observation of physical phenomena which owe the origins of their present state to events which happened in those same prehistoric times.

In each case there are, I think, some undeniable concurrences. 1. The stones are there, and one can derive inference from, or speculation about them. 2. The stories in which folk interpretation is expressed take much the same form, and so may have migrated, and become attached to the local sites, overlaying or replacing genuine folk memory, perhaps as a way of expressing that in a form amenable to oral recording. 3. An idea common to the human condition can be conveyed by this process, which makes it the more durable and so preserves it, for probably long successive periods of human generations.

This balance between fact and fable lies at the heart of our subject matter here, the investigation of the story and the stones of Llys Helig; of my understanding of the nature of myth; and of the underlying structure of this book.

We have, at this stage, that most interesting of situations, a paradox, a dichotomy, an ambiguity. Which of the two versions will in the end stand up may, in the end, be indeterminate. Can it perhaps be both? Can an account in fact be both fanciful and factual, and if so how are we to understand it? Perhaps we shall see, in due course; perhaps not.

Perhaps we shall simply be left with a beautiful mystery.

Part of the lesson learnt, in any case, is that things like this are not so simple. The power of myth, as of poetry, lies in its ability to display more than one dimension at the same time. Such is its nature, and in such lies its fascination.

V The View from Mount Ararat

'Stories about the flood,' writes Alan H.F. Griffin, in his paper 'Ovid's Universal Flood', (in a Trinity College Dublin Review published in 1992), 'can be divided into two types – universal and local.' He, of course, as his title states, is writing about the universal one.

Ovid's is the best and fullest version of the story of the survival of Deucalion, and his wife Pyrrha, of a flood sent by Jove to wipe out the human race, because of its iniquity.

In Ovid's *Metamorphoses* he tells us of a time when the 'Golden Age' was over. An age in which material acquisition and consequent violence, war and crime, had taken over, had distressed and angered Jove, the king of the gods. After calling a Council of the other deities, he announced his decision to wipe out the entire human race. By means of torrential rain and overflowing rivers he flooded the land, until 'sea and earth could no longer be distinguished: all was sea, and a sea that had no shore . . . '

Ovid describes the attempt of the population to avoid this – 'some tried to escape by climbing to the hilltops' – but in his story only one couple did, on Mount Parnassus:

When the waters had covered all the rest of the earth, the little boat which carried Deucalion and his wife ran aground here.

Their survival, although in this case not planned, was due to their exemption from the general sinfulness:

> Of all the men who ever lived, Deucalion was the best and the most upright, no woman ever showed more reverence for the gods than Pyrrha, his wife.

The flood declines, but everything has changed. When Deucalion 'saw the desolate lands all deeply silent, tears started to his eyes . . . '

Ovid was writing in Latin at the turn of the era, about the time of the birth of Christ. He had a Greek source, and the story was known in Greece some centuries before. Pindar, for instance, writing in the 5th century B.C., refers to it in his ninth Olympian ode.

> . . . For they say
> the black earth was awash
> under the weight of water; but by
> Zeus' means, of a sudden the ebb-tide
> drained the flood. And from these
> came your ancestors . . .

There is of course something very familiar about this, the flood covering the world and the survivors coming to land in a boat; and indeed Griffin's project is to trace the parallels between Ovid and Genesis. He quotes M.L. West, from his work *Hesiod Works and Days*, as saying 'Greece's oriental contacts in the eighth century were primarily Semitic', and that the story, which (West says) 'of course' came from the east, got attached to Deucalion simply because in Greek mythology Deucalion was the first man.

Indeed the parallels between Ovid and Genesis are sufficient to convince us of an ultimate common origin, if not of direct borrowing of the Greek source from the Semitic. Jove reacts to what he sees on earth by groaning aloud, and shortly 'his heart swelled with dreadful wrath'. When 'God saw that the wickedness of man was great in the earth' he repents of his creation, and 'it grieved him at his heart'. In Ovid the flood is such that the hills were overwhelmed and waves washed the peaks. In Genesis 'all the high hills' were covered. In both version there is one exception to this: Parnassus and Ararat remain uncovered – and it is on those peaks that the boat carrying the protagonist comes to rest. Deucalion is saved because he 'was the best and most upright' of all men; Noah 'found grace in the eyes of the Lord' because he 'was a just man and perfect in his generations' and he 'walked with God'. The survivors in each case are given the task of repopulating the earth.

Griffin also finds links between Ovid and another part of Genesis, that which recounts the destruction of Sodom and Gomorrah, the 'cities of the Plain'. From our point of view it may be noted that although God 'rained' on them fire and brimstone instead of water, these cities are said, in Chapter 14, to lie under the Dead Sea; and in this case too there was a chosen group of survivors, Lot and his daughters.

Griffin quotes West as saying that the Greek and later Latin version is 'nothing but the story of Ziusudra-Utnapishtim-Noah, transferred to the improbable setting of central Greece'. Noah, in other words, is not the ultimate or singular origin of this story.

G.S. Kirk, Professor of Classics at the University of Cambridge, has argued persuasively for the derivation of the flood-myth, and other Greek themes, from the Middle East, and specifically Mesopotamia. In his book *The Nature of Greek Myths* he points out that wide-spread flooding was not a feature of Greek experience (though perhaps forgetting, as we can not, the *tsunami* resulting from the eruption of Santorini), whereas the Euphrates, fed by the snows of the mountains of western Anatolia, periodically overwhelmed the settlements built along its banks, until this problem was solved by the construction of drainage channels and irrigation canals in the second millennium B.C. That these events were intermittent rather than regular is shown by the fact that the cities were built again in the same places, giving rise to stratified mounds in which excavation can clearly uncover different, and dateable, habitation levels. Kirk says that the Greeks would not have got their flood-myth from Egypt: the Nile flooded every year, and the flood was benign, bringing fertility. At the city of Ur in Mesopotamia archaeologists found the evidence of one particularly cataclysmic flood in the form of a layer of mud a remarkable three to four metres thick, dateable to about 3500 B.C., which it is tempting to see as the archetypal great flood of the myth.

Because in Mesopotamia mankind had been particularly created by the gods to serve them, rather than, as in Greece, being almost in the role of the gods' colleagues, it was natural that if they failed they should be destroyed; and indeed the theme of the anger of the gods at human weakness underlies the Mesopotamian flood story. One version of this is an Akkadian poem in which a sole commendable individual, Atra-hasis, is permitted to survive. In Sumerian poems the survivor is named as Ziusudra. The best flood story of all, and the one which Kirk sees as diffusing the theme throughout the Middle East in the 3rd millennium B.C., is central to the Epic of Gilgamesh, at least in its final form in Akkadian, inscribed in cuneiform writing on twelve tablets from the library of the Assyrian king Assurbanipal, who reigned from 668 to 627 B.C. These tablets were rediscovered in the mid 19th century in the course of the investigation of the Assyrian city mounds.

'Gilgamesh' was first written down in the early second millennium B.C., but it is thought to belong in origin to the third. Gilgamesh reports on his travels, in search of fame and immortality, and on what he has learnt of 'the time before the flood'. In the course of his wanderings he finds Utnapishtim, the only survivor of the flood, who tells Gilgamesh the story.

The gods agree to exterminate mankind, which has become too numerous and unruly. Utnapishtim is warned in a dream and told to build a boat, for which he is given detailed specifications. He is told to take into it 'the seed of all living creatures'. He builds the boat and stocks it, boards it when the rains come. Thunder and deluge lead to the bursting of dams and dykes. The storm lasts six days and the flood 'overwhelmed the world'. On the seventh it calms, and Utnapishtim looks out and sees 'on every side the waste of water'. His boat grounds on a single exposed mountain. After six days he lets loose a dove, which returns, finding no resting place. A swallow also comes back. When he looses a raven it finds carrion and stays, showing the waters have retreated.

The relation between this story and that of Noah, evident in the details of the boat and the sending of birds, has already been referred to; N.K. Sandars, the translator of the Penguin 'Gilgamesh', says in her Introduction: 'The opinion, at one time widely held, that the Genesis account was a late refinement on a story once current in all the cities of Babylonia, is not now so general; while the view that it derives directly from a very old and independent history has many supporters . . . at present the Genesis account is probably best seen against a background of many very ancient flood stories not necessarily relating to the same disaster, and with different protagonists, both human and divine.' It is impossible to resist the temptation to remark that we are in danger of getting into deep water.

It is tempting to see these Near Eastern examples as the roots of the European flood stories, spreading along familiar trade routes westwards. Even the Norse theme of Ragnarok, the cataclysmic end of the world, in which the World Serpent will lash the sea against the land and 'earth will sink in the sea' may owe something to these apparently earlier examples. There are of course alternatives to the idea of dissemination by contact, one of which is that, if you are going to envisage the total destruction of the world there is not a lot of option. As H.R. Ellis Davidson put it in her book *Gods and Myths of Northern Europe*, while criticising the tendency to draw parallels between Christianity and Norse mythology: 'It is obvious that if one contemplates the destruction of the world, whether in a religious context or not, certain possibilities are bound to occur to the mind. Destruction by intense heat and cold and inundation by water are likely to be among them.' That is one way of looking at the question of the common elements, which we might call the psychological angle. There is as usual the alternative, the appeal to experience. Michael Jordan expresses this attitude in the chapter 'Myths of Apocalypse, Fire and Flood' in his *Myths of the World*: 'One has to ponder on why so many cultures envisage a great flood or deluge having taken place sometime during their early history. The notions of the underground primeval waters which will rise again to engulf a sinful and errant humankind is universal. Perhaps it can be accounted for most simply by the fact that many parts of the world at one time or another experienced great inundations either through the flooding of river valleys, or tidal waves, or encroachment by the sea.'

One feature which is not so easy to explain by appeal to imaginative limitations or to early losses of coastal settlements is the constant, almost universal, implication of guilt. The gods decide to exterminate humanity because of its transgressions; or some particular society has fallen into decadent ways, and will face the consequences. Sometimes this transgression takes the form of a single wrong act, as we saw earlier in the cases of maidens who left the well lid off. In the Irish case of the sacred well of Nechtan, for instance, from the Mythological Cycle, a flood was caused by the breaking of a taboo. Nor is this theme by any means confined to the European examples. In the Hindu tale of Varaha (the incarnation of Vishnu as a boar) so much damage is being done by him to the earth that the gods appeal to the creator, Narayana, who causes total inundation.

The theme is popular too in the Americas. The Hopi Indians have a story that the decadence of the people caused the water to rise from the underworld, and the Algonquin, more particularly, tell how the mythic character Nanabush (visualised as the Great Hare) killed some of the Underwater Panthers, the rest of whom in retaliation brought a great flood, swamping the earth. The Navajo have the flood being caused by a water-monster, Tieholtsodi, upset at the theft by the first people of his children. He was eventually placated by their return, and the flood subsided before it had caused complete destruction. The agent of the universal flood in the lore of the Crees is a different sort of character, the familiar trickster figure here called Wisagatcak, who caused it in the course of his pursuit of a monstrous beaver. He escaped it himself on a raft, onto which he took various types of animal.

Further south the Incas have Viracocha, the creator god, destroying all the people except two, partly by a great flood which rose above the highest mountains, because they had become disobedient. Viracocha is pictured in some versions as having emerged alone from Lake Titicaca, after the flood subsided, to found the human race.

The *Popol Vuh*, the sacred book of the ancient Quiche Maya, of the Guatemalan highlands, was written, in the Quiche tongue, after the Maya had been taught to read and write by the Spanish, and so the possibility of direct influence from Christianity cannot be discounted. But anyone who has read the *Popol Vuh* will know that its tone and imagery proclaim an authentic tradition conveyed by someone who cared deeply about it: so when we read that the first race of wooden men 'did not remember their Creator' and 'no longer remembered the Heart of Heaven and therefore they fell out of favor' we recognise, I think, a native theme. 'A flood was brought about by the Heart of Heaven; a great flood was formed which fell on the heads of the wooden creatures.' The editors of the English version, Delia Goetz and Sylvanus Morley, comment in a note:

> The idea of a flood in olden times and the belief in another which would be the end of the world . . . still existed among the Indians of Guatemala in the years following the Spanish conquest.

This is perhaps something of an understatement. Flood stories are everywhere in South America, even today. Bochica, a major god of the Colombian Indians, had a rival called Chibchacum, who attempted in his anger to destroy the people of the Bogota plain by sending a great flood. They appealed to Bochica, who saved them by drying and draining the waters. The equivalent saviour in the lore of the Araucanian Indians of Chile is Guinechen, who saved mankind from a flood caused by an evil power. Of course it is impossible to say to what extent these Latin American sources are influenced by Christian teaching.

Another theme which seems to crop up independently in these far-flung places, and which relates the world myth to our own coastal waters, is the element of the survivor-to-be being warned in advance. Helig ignored the warning, being misled; and in some cases he or his counterparts are not saved, only the harpist and in some cases the cellar-boy.

The Huichol Indians live in Sierra Madre, north-east of the Rio Grande. They have a story in which a man felling trees to make room for cultivation is warned by an old woman with magical powers that a great flood is coming in five days; he is to make a box and get into it, taking with him grains of corn. When the flood comes he drifts in this for four years, and in the fifth comes to rest on the top of a mountain. A long way away, in India, the story of Manu occurs in ancient Brahmanic writings. Manu is warned by Visnu in the form of a fish to build a boat, because a great flood is coming which will destroy the first created world. He thus comes to be the sole survivor, and hence the ancestor of mankind.

The people of the Americas are not the only group to have had a particular obsession with the flood theme. It occurs early in Chinese creation myth, and crops up in several central stories. Perhaps because the influence of European conquerors is missing here the Chinese version shows a slightly different structural pattern, but it is still a matter of destruction of the world by flood. In one creation story the monster Gong-gong, failing in an attempt to sieze power, tilted the earth and caused the rivers to flood. In another story connected with the emperor Yao the floods reached as far as the sky. The emperor sought the help of Gun, a mythic hero, who built dams. His task was thwarted, but in the end completed by his son Yu.

No doubt there are many more instances of flood stories to be found in the world's mythologies; but these above are enough to demonstrate that destruction by inundation is a world-wide image, and is often seen in the same form as our home story of Llys Helig: a warning, retribution for transgression, a surviving individual or couple, and the past world gone.

In Europe, from classical times until now, the one image which seems best to encapsulate this theme and which still holds our perennial attention is that of Atlantis.

VI Locating Atlantis

Spyridon Marinatos, then Emeritus Professor of Archeology at the University of Athens, opens his little book *Some Words About the Legend of Atlantis* by pointing out that 'over two thousand books and publications . . . have been issued on the subject of Atlantis'. That was in 1971 (though the words probably belong to a paper written in 1950). Hardly a month goes by without a new theory appearing in the catalogues of the mail-order book clubs, tying the idea of a lost civilisation to that ancient image. Atlantis is the paradigm of the lost ideal world.

The story of Atlantis comes to us through two of Plato's Dialogues, the *Critias* and the *Timaeus*, in both of which Critias recounts it to Socrates. It is, we are assured, 'not a mere legend, but an actual fact'.

Interestingly, from our point of view, a generational structure is built into the provenance of the story. It was the respected statesman and poet Solon, in the sixth century B.C. (he died about 558), who learnt the story on a trip to Egypt. Solon was a friend of Critias' great-grandfather, and he told the story to the latter's son, also called Critias. He in due course repeated it to his grandchildren, 'an old-world story which I heard from an aged man'. At the time Critias the elder was ninety, and the one now telling the story to Socrates was ten. This is the brief account of Atlantis, as given in the *Timaeus*.

Solon, in Egypt, discussed antiquity with the learned

priests, and seeking to impress them told them about the Deluge, and the survival of Deucalion and Pyrrha. One very aged priest dismissed this as a comparatively recent tradition, and told of a far older one. 'In the first place you remember a single deluge only, but there were many previous ones . . . ' He speaks of a time 'before the great deluge of all', some nine thousand years ago.

The Athens of that time was attacked by a mighty power which 'came forth out of the Atlantic Ocean', from an island 'larger than Libya and Asia put together' which lay 'in front of the straits which are by you called the pillars of Heracles'. 'Now in this island of Atlantis there was a great and wonderful empire' which had subjected much of Europe and northern Africa. Athens alone withstood this subjugation.

> But afterwards there occurred violent earthquakes and floods; and in a single day and night of misfortune all your warlike men in a body sank into the earth, and the island of Atlantis in like manner disappeared in the depths of the sea. For which reason the sea in those parts is impassable and impenetrable, because there is a shoal of mud in the way; and this was caused by the subsidence of the island.

In the *Critias* the eponymous narrator gives a more detailed description of Atlantis – its fertile plain, its central citadel, its dynasty, descended from Poseidon, its great wealth. In due course this abundance has a debasing effect, the population 'becoming tainted with unrighteous ambition and power'. Zeus perceived this, 'and wanting to inflict punishment on them that they might be chastened' called a conference of the gods. Tantalisingly just before he announces his decision the unfinished *Critias* breaks off. It is a fair assumption that had

Plato finished the Dialogue he would have had Zeus deciding to send the 'violent earthquakes and floods' which in the *Timaeus* Critias remembered being told that Solon said caused the submergence of Atlantis.

Thirty-two years before he published his little booklet, *Some Words About The Legend of Atlantis*, an article by Spyridon Marinatos had appeared in the British journal *Antiquity*, in the December 1939 edition, entitled 'The Volcanic Destruction of Minoan Crete'. He was already by then the Director of the Greek Archeological Service.

In the article Marinatos argues that the wholesale destruction of the Minoan cities of Crete must have been caused by an exceptional event. Somewhat arbitrarily he plumps for the great eruption of Thera (now known as Santorini), which was thought to have taken place in about 1500 B.C. By comparison with the recorded eruption of Krakatoa in 1883 he concludes that among the devastating physical effects of this event 'worst of all was a series of terrific waves which rose after the explosion'. He reasons that the waves which struck Crete after Santorini exploded would have been even greater than those which pounded Java and Sumatra in 1883. Notably he does not point to archeological evidence for destruction by flood; everything in the Cretan palaces was found as it was when in use – 'Huge double axes, the sacred symbols, lay where they had fallen . . . At Gournia the carpenter's and coppersmith's shops were found intact' – whereas one might have expected it all to be washed up against walls. At Amnisos he found 'a great mass of pumice and sand'. He also found evidence of destruction by fire. 'This was a great problem,' he admits candidly, 'as I could not reconcile the fire with a terrible inundation caused by the sea.' Determined not to let the facts spoil his theory, Marinatos presses on: the waves knocked over the oil lamps, which set the houses on fire. Quite how this happened when they were presumably under water may puzzle us, but apparently something similar took place at Krakatoa.

The fact that most of the palace-cities of Minoan Crete were too elevated for even the greatest *tsunami* to reach them, and they were equally suddenly destroyed, is another minor difficulty. Marinatos speculates that the eruption of Santorini would have been followed by earthquakes, and it was these which brought the palaces down. The *tsunami* theory is not abandoned, but can only be selectively used.

It is odd that it is to this tentative and inconclusive paper that the connection of Atlantis with Minoan Crete owes its modern origins, particularly as at this time Marinatos does not seem to have thought of it himself. The editors of *Antiquity* append a disclaimer, to the effect that 'the main thesis of this article requires additional support from excavation'. This is quoted by Sir Mortimer Wheeler at the start of his Preface to J.V. Luce's book *The End of Atlantis*, where he points out that then, thirty years later, Marinatos was in the process of carrying out excavations at Akrotiri, on Santorini itself. Spectacular as his findings have been the revealing of a Minoan town at Akrotiri does not provide grounds for equating either Santorini itself or the Minoan world in general with Atlantis. Yet since that is what so many people have done, we must begin to wonder why. From our immediate point of view this question is important since it concerns the widespread desire to place the site of a legend in both the geographical and historical worlds.

Although perhaps Marinatos was not aware of it at the time, since his article connects Crete with the Santorini eruption but not with Atlantis, the idea that Minoan Crete might have been the original Atlantis had first appeared –

with no reference to Santorini – in an anonymous article in *The Times*, of 19th February, 1909. The inspiration for this was the wealth of finds in the Minoan palaces. The author turned out to be K.T. Frost, who returned to the subject in more detail in the *Journal of Hellenic Studies*, with a paper entitled 'The *Critias* and Minoan Crete'. Frost's arguments do not stand up to rigorous analysis. Minoan Crete was wealthy; Atlantis was wealthy; Minoan Crete came to an abrupt end at the height of its power (which Frost attributes to invasion); so did legendary Atlantis. Therefore they are the same place. This sort of reasoning is accepted by those who want a tidy location for Atlantis, such as E.V. Luce, who says that the article makes its case 'with such conciseness and cogency' that it is surprising it was not taken more seriously.

Luce's book appeared in 1969, fuelled by the Santorini excavations, and the same year saw the publication of a book written jointly by the distinguished seismologist Professor A. Galanopoulos and the archaeologist Edward Bacon, entitled provocatively *Atlantis, The Truth Behind the Legend*. By the time Marinatos published his 1971 booklet (a reprint, with a new Preface, of a 1950 paper) he seems to have come to accept much of the later theorising to which his 1939 article had accidentally given rise. 'I continue to believe . . . that the eruption of Thera may be the raison d'être to the Atlantis literature.'

The trouble with trying to fit Atlantis into the Mediterranean is that you have to accept certain details given by Plato while rejecting others. You have to hold, for instance, that he was right about the wealth, power and advanced civilisation, but wrong about its size, date and location. This is simply unreasonable, as it could just as well be the other way round. The dates of the occurrences also needed a bit of manipulation, since the explosion was reckoned to have taken place about 1500 B.C., whereas Minoan civilisation is normally reckoned to have ended about 1450. All such theories are now outdated, since tree-ring analysis produced in 1988 ties the date of the eruption precisely to 1628 B.C., a date supported by the evidence of acidic ash in the ice cores of Greenland, much too early to be the cause of the Cretan decline. Moreover even in 1969, at the height of the Atlantis speculation, Norman Hammond, archaeological correspondent to *The Times*, dismissed the *tsunami* theory: a sonar survey of the Santorini caldera showed that 'its configuration is such that *tsunami* formation would be markedly inhibited at source, and that in any case the main force of any *tsunami* resulting from the eruption would be directed not towards Crete, but N.N.W. towards the Peloponnese'. This, he says, explains why there is no evidence of destruction by tidal wave at the Minoan sites.

Early writers on the subject tended to follow Plato geographically. Ignatius Donnelly, who published *Atlantis: The Antediluvian World* in New York in 1882, sets it firmly in the Atlantic, and his follower Lewis Spence related the lost land to existing island groups, in three books published in the 1920's.

With the obsessive literalism which seems to dog Atlantis theory, several writers are keen to show why it could not have been in the Atlantic. Galanopoulos and Bacon say ' . . . there is no sunken landmass in the Atlantic; the Atlantic Ocean must have existed in its present form for at least a million years'. Luce admits that there is a mid-Atlantic Ridge, which comes to the surface occasionally as in the Azores, Ascension Island, and Tristan da Cunha. But this is thought to have been raised from the ocean floor, not to have sunk beneath its surface. He says that if the scientific opinion is sound 'we must give up the notion of locating Atlantis as a lost continent in the middle of the North Atlantic'. More recently Graham Hancock, in his book *Fingerprints of the Gods* points out that modern oceanographers have 'thoroughly mapped the floor of the Atlantic Ocean and there was definitely no lost continent lurking there'. One begins to wonder why they are not content to conclude that Plato was dealing in poetic imagery, and placed his island in the Atlantic because there was room for it there. Yet everyone concerned with the matter is desperate to find a geographical home for Atlantis.

Recently – perhaps a sign of an apparent tendency at this time to seek a literal interpretation of myth – there have been attempts to show that Atlantis was in fact where Plato said it was, right opposite and just outside the Strait of Gibraltar.

Marinatos' literalism is selective: he takes Plato as being right in saying that the Athenian army was destroyed at the same time as the island, but wrong, because it is inconsistent with this, in placing the latter in the Atlantic. He operates a similar attitude towards the date, calling the nine thousand years before Solon a 'colossal anachronism' for the time of a metal-working, politically organised people, without saying why Plato might have been right about the date, wrong about the metal-working and so on. 'The legend as it stands cannot be accepted': but why then seek to make part of it historical?

It is the same syndrome which we have seen many times already, from Llys Helig's attribution to the sixth century, which people try to prove or dispute, and which we shall have to think about further in connection with the whole business of the relationship of myth to history. In the meantime there continue to be further and ever more ludicrous attempts to place Atlantis in time and space.

Hancock himself, publishing in 1995 his closely argued but often bizarre work about a long-lost super-race, concludes that Atlantis now lies under the Antarctic ice. His reasons include the fact that there is nowhere else he can think of where it could be. He blames its demise on a 'massive displacement of the earth's crust', which shifted it 2000 miles south.

Even as this book goes to print, early in 2002, Hancock is involved in a project labelled the Asian Atlantis, investigating what appears to be a large built complex three miles off the west coast of India, in 120 feet of water in the Gulf of Khambhat. Tests on recovered artefacts indicate a provisional date of 7,500 B.C., supporting his theories recently set out in a new book that civilisation started 5,000 years earlier than previously thought but was widely lost by rising seas at the end of the last Ice Age.

One of the more recent theories about Atlantis brings us back to Lyonesse, since it places it on the Celtic Shelf about a hundred miles off Land's End, identifying it with a maritime feature known as Little Sole Bank. A Russian classical scholar led a twenty-strong team of divers in search of evidence in the summer of 1998. That the Celtic Shelf was a fertile plain which was flooded by the ice melt at the end of the last ice age is agreed by experts to be probable. It is the insistence that Little Sole Bank fits Plato's description of the capital of Atlantis that is perplexing. Why, we begin to wonder, does every putative lost civilisation nowadays have to conform to Plato's specifications? Why is Plato's pleasant fable to be taken as Holy Writ?

The latest and perhaps the most outlandish attempt to locate Atlantis has it 12,000 feet up in Bolivia. In the true spirit of British exploration, and with a name to match it, Colonel John Blashford-Snell set off in the spring of 1998 to investigate Lake Poopo, where he believed was the remains of a civilisation that lived on a big island in the middle of the lake, wiped out by a volcano. 'This fits many of the criteria for Atlantis,' he pointed out, and added rather unexpectedly 'and might also explain how traces of tobacco and cocaine, products of this region, ended up in ancient Egyptian mummies.'

Blashford-Snell's expedition was partly the fruit of fourteen years of investigation by an amateur archeologist from Torquay. Jim Allen spent this time trying to match Plato's description with natural features shown on aerial and satellite photography. Just as the Russian expert took a team of twenty to the Scilly Isles, and at about the same time, these West Country enthusiasts turned their backs on their homeland and took a team of twenty, again, six thousand miles away to Lake Poopo. It was described by *The Sunday Times* at the time as 'one of the least likely expeditions in the history of British exploration'. Blashford-Snell was undeterred: there were at least fifty factors, he claimed, corresponding between Bolivia and Plato's description. These turn out to be rather general – both have islands, both have plains – but it is this astonishing determination to deal literally with Plato that must surprise us.

Such bizarre excursions as that of Blashford-Snell point to what I think is a basic error underlying the whole business of locating Atlantis, or Lyonesse, or Cantre'r Gwaelod, or Llys Helig: quite regardless of what may or may not have happened in coastal regions, lakes or inland plains, in pre-history or geological time, these named places are located in international fable, and as such they are not to be found on the earth's surface, even under its waters, but in the broad fertile territory of the mind. This is not to deny the relation of the fable to real once-experienced events – but to distinguish, while admitting the possible relation, between the two. The group of stones which lies under the water of Conwy Bay a mile off the shore of Penmaenmawr may once have been associated with human activity. Llys Helig on the other hand is a wonderful thought, a fertile and enticing district in the land of the imagination. To go there is unnecessary. You are there already.

VII Myth and History

It was a hot day in Latium. The Emperor of Rome rested from his hunting about the middle of the day. His staff built a canopy of shields on spears above him, and he slept. He dreamt.

He dreams he has sailed to a far country, and crossing it comes to a mountainous seaboard, where a castle stands by the mouth of a river. Going in he sees a beautiful girl, and he falls in love.

At that point the restless movements of the dogs and horses wakes him, but the infatuation aroused in the dream has not evaporated with it. He pines, and is obliged to send out men in search of his dream-lady. Eventually they come to the island of Britain and find her in a castle in Arfon. She will not go to Rome, so the Emperor comes to her.

The Emperor (named as Macsen) builds strongholds for her at Caernarfon, Caerleon and Carmarthen *(Caerfyrddin)*. She (named Elen in the story) instigates the construction of roads between the fortresses. An idyllic seven years comes to an end when a rival emperor is proclaimed in Rome, and Macsen takes an army from Britain to combat him. He succeeds, and many of the British he took with him stay in Italy.

In January of the year 388 an army led by Magnus Maximus including many men from Britain assaulted Rome. Maximus was a Spanish adventurer serving in the Roman army in Britain, where his success in leadership and popularity with the legions led to his being proclaimed Emperor, partly in protest at the incompetent and expensive rule of Gratian. He took his largely British army to France, in the process severely depleting the garrisons in places like Caernarfon, and in effect ending the period of Roman rule in such regions. The Romans who left did not come back.

Of course the Romans did not first come to Britain because the Emperor fell in love in a dream, nor were they here for merely seven years, but many of the ingredients of this attractive fable are real enough. The hero, for instance, Macsen, clearly developed from the usurping Maximus; the taking of the army to the continent and the assault on Rome are almost literal memories of real events of his reign. The roads and forts are still there to be seen, and no doubt were in more substantial shape when the story was first constructed. The empress Elen, associated with the building of the roads, was a memory of Helena, wife of Constantius and mother of Constantine, both emperors associated with the Roman roads of Britain. Indeed one of these still bears her name, Sarn Elen, the main north-south Roman route in Wales, which runs from Caerhun in the Conwy valley to Carmarthen in South Wales.

This *Mabinogion* tale, 'The Dream of Macsen Wledig', illustrates, in fact, the ways in which history becomes transformed in myth. There are, to begin with, elements of international popular tales, perhaps the function of which is to make a story memorable. Such formulae would clearly aid transmission of the material in the oral tradition, as well as add to its popularity with its audience. Falling in love in a dream is one such ingredient. Kenneth Jackson points out, in his book *The International Popular Tale and Early Welsh Tradition*, (the 1961 Gregynog Lecture), that the beginning of 'Macsen' is reminiscent of Lucian's account of Medea's falling in love with Jason in a dream, 'and is familiar in Sanskrit literature and early Irish . . . It is told in Scottish Gaelic as the opening of the story about the sinking of the Spanish Armada galleon in Tobermory harbour'.

From our point of view, taking a hard look at the legend of Llys Helig, certain features of the comparison of Macsen's story with Maximus' help us to see what is happening. A series of real events – the Romans coming to Britain, their rule and constructions there, their eventual departure – have become compressed into a single episode. Diverse historical characters – Magnus Maximus and the Empress Helena – have become conjoined. The time of many emperors has become reduced to that of one, Macsen, and the whole theme of Rome in Britain represented by him. A general structure is retained, in fact, but in simplified form, with much detail omitted.

The same thing happened, in British myth, with the tales of King Arthur. Tentative references by early historians became worked up during the Middle Ages into a full-blown romantic myth-cycle. Themes from all over the corpus of myth became attracted into this field – giants, deities, magic animals, enchantresses, impossible tasks, endless quests – and figures at first quite independent come to join the throng at Arthur's court. Merlin, Lancelot, Morgan le Faye, Perceval, Gawain – they all originated as heroes or deities in their own right, but all got sucked into orbit around the Arthurian nucleus. So too, on our own shores, we have seen Helig and Gwyddno becoming associated without much reason, along with the great Taliesin, with Maelgwn Gwynedd, and the whole thing settled in time, like Arthur's story, in a vaguely medieval world supposed to have occurred (where there was historical room for it) in the sixth century.

History shows the probability of a historical counterpart to the legendary Arthur. According to *The Anglo-Saxon Chronicle* something appears to have gone wrong with the Anglo-Saxon advance between the years 514 and 547. Two separate sources also record that Angles were returning to the continent in large numbers during the 530s. There may have been many attempts at this time to resist the flood-tide of Saxon invasion, and there may have been many military heroes leading them. We know for instance of Ambrosius, who revived hope in a national revival. The whole matter, no doubt complicated, somehow became summarised, compressed, personalised, and given the name of Arthur. Dressed up then in the panoply of traditional heroic themes, with familiar figures playing supporting roles, a critical time of history became a national myth.

This is a familiar process, and I think it tells us much about Helig. E.V. Luce, for instance, in the book referred to in the last chapter, has a section called 'The historical element in Greek myths and legends', in which he shows how archaeological excavation has shown the basic accuracy of Homer's geographical allocation of the events of the Trojan war and the travels of Odysseus. It is interesting for us to find that although the Trojan war and the Mycenean world in which it took place were five hundred years in the past when Homer composed his works, he seems to have got much of it, even in detail, right.

Nora Chadwick, in her book *The British Heroic Age*, points out how attitudes have been changed by modern scholarship. 'Early scholars held our heroic records, especially heroic epics such as the *Iliad*, for fiction.' The scholars of our time have come to recognise that in these works 'we have oral records which reflect genuine history'. She points however to an important feature, which we too must bear in mind. In the process of the conversion of fact into fable a strange distortion has taken place, particularly in the viewing of the process of causality. Just as perhaps many generals have been run into one, in the person of Agamemnon, or Arthur, so too the matter has become deeply personalised. Our modern scholars have come to 'the realisation that the true basis of the Trojan War was not Helen's beauty, but an economic cause. It lay in the soil of Greece, which was too thin to be self-supporting, and on the other hand the wealth of Asia Minor in corn. The cause of the war was hunger, but the heroic poet attributes it to Helen's beauty'.

Asking why this is, Chadwick points to a mainly aesthetic motive. It is the function of the court bard to entertain. His audience 'has no interest in political conceptions, economic conditions, national boundaries or city life'. They want to hear about 'personal heroes and their feats of valour, their tragic deaths . . . '

One Welsh myth which is often cited as being relevant to our present investigation is the story of Branwen. The *Mabinogion* tale 'Branwen, daughter of Llŷr' probably dates in its present structure from the early eleventh century but, like all the traditional Welsh material, belongs to early medieval recording of ancient oral lore which may of course date back thousands of years. It contains a statement which indicates a knowledge of coastal change which has, like the Mycenean archaeology which parallels Homer, found geological support in recent times. At some point in the story Bran takes his army to Ireland. ' . . . and in those days the deep water was not wide. He went by wading. There were but two rivers, the Lli and the Archan were they called, but thereafter the deep water grew wider when the deep overflowed the kingdoms.' The time when Britain and

Ireland were only separated by rivers was, however, most probably during the Pleistocene age, which ended about ten thousand years ago. Recent, in geological time; but a long spell, we cannot help thinking, over which to remember former geographical details.

This however is exactly what seems to be taking place in the cases of these myths of flood. In the late 1990s two marine geologists at Columbia University in New York produced a book called *Noah's Flood*, which put forward the theory that the Biblical (and hence classical) 'great flood' was a memory of the breaking through of the Mediterranean into the Black Sea. This led Dr Robert Ballard, discoverer of deep-sea wrecks such as the Titanic and the Bismarck, to take an expedition there in 1999. According to Ballard some 7,600 years ago the rising level of the Mediterranean caused by the melting of the ice at the end of the last Ice Age gave rise to a breakthrough of the ridge separating the two at the Bosphorus, the Black Sea then being a much smaller freshwater lake. 'People living there are four hundred feet below sea level,' he told the *Sunday Times*. 'They are facing a flood equal to 10,000 Niagara Falls.' Ballard claimed to have discovered evidence of the ancient coastline at a depth of 450 feet. By September 2000, better equipped, they had found what they took to be evidence of human habitation: an apparently wattle-and-daub structure, bits of pottery, and some tools, which they took at first to be made of stone but which, rather mysteriously, turned out when samples were retrieved to be wooden. Unfortunately when the dispatches ended in October 2000 no samples had by then been dated, and since news of the results does not seem to have been made public we are not in a position to draw any firm conclusions either way.

From our point of view, thinking about the sudden

flooding of Helig's kingdom, the Black Sea hypothesis is of particular interest. Unlike coastal erosion or the gradual rising of sea-levels over fertile plains it would represent a sudden and (literally) overwhelming catastrophe. 'If the American scientists' theory is correct,' *The Times* comments in an editorial, 'although the Book of Genesis might embroider the story, it records an actual event.'

The Times is probably oversimplifying in allocating the world's flood myths to that one cataclysmic inundation of the Black Sea. The Mediterranean basin itself has undergone considerable variations in its relation of water to land, as is evidenced by the poignant sight of the bones of several now-extinct species crowded into a cave on the island of Malta, once evidently part of a rock-ridge which formed the last refuge of these rejects from Noah's Ark.

It is odd, in view of the consistency of the relation of myth to history – that of a summary form, a compression – that those who wish to demean the status of a myth or legend seek to show that it is unhistorical. So, for instance, North, whose programme was to undermine the story of Llys Helig, seeks to show that there was no inundation in Conwy Bay in the sixth century. There is no mention of it in the early sources – the *Annales*, the *Brut y Tywysogyon*, *The Anglo-Saxon Chronicles*, Gildas, Nennius, Roger of Wendover. The earliest references to Helig are in a genealogy published in the *Bonedd y Saint* in the 13th century, and to his inundation – *'gwyr heuyt a oresgynwys mor eu tir'*, and *'gwyr a orysgynnod mor eu tir'* – in the 1455 copy. None of the early references to Helig's land say that it was in Conwy Bay. The whole thing is therefore fiction, and the stones have a purely geological origin. 'It is not a case of trying to show that there is no literary evidence for an occurrence that we know could not have taken place; there can, of course, be no such evidence.' This over-simplification is based on the supposition, which is easily disposable, that the story has to be taken literally. Treat it as a fanciful way of encapsulating a sequence too complex for easy recording, and it is perfectly possible to hold that occurrences of the form referred to did take place, and therefore that the site of the myth may have been the site of real examples of them. We shall consider in the next chapter the evidence which could support a theory as to whether or not this is the case.

One of the reasons some people seem determined to take a committed position in relation to mythic material is that the word 'myth' has acquired an implication which it does not bear for me. To many people it seems to mean 'false' or 'fictional', and so it cannot be compatible with history. Think of it however as meaning 'symbolically true', and one can see that myth and history are simply two different views of the same thing. Writing about John Barton's epic nine-play cycle *Tantalus*, the *Sunday Times* theatre critic John Peter sums this point up: 'Mythology is the psychological version of history'. The same thing is seen from two different perspectives, and in the process certain things about it come to look quite different. It is the same sort of difference as exists between the 'mind' and the 'brain'. Take, for instance – a matter we touched on earlier – mythic and historic approaches to causality. As Nora Chadwick remarked in relation to the causes of the Trojan War, the matter has become personalised, in the myth. It has become the mental, humanised counterpart of the objective sequence.

These are not perspectives of the sort that one may be wrong and the other right. They are two ways of seeing and describing the same thing, as it were from the inside and then the outside.

The difference in viewpoint results on the one hand in the

idea of human transgression causing the anger of a deity, who determines to destroy the transgressors by sending a flood – and on the other hand the concept of melt-water from retreating ice breaking through a rock ridge and submerging a fertile plain. Because we live in a scientific time we tend to allot primary value to the hard physical facts; but this should not lead us to belittle in any way their psychological, subjective counterpart. As Sir John Rhys put it, in *Celtic Folklore*: seen 'as a reality to those who believed in them, the superstitions of our ancestors form an integral part of this history (and) it is a mark of an uncultured people not to know, or care to know about the history of the race'.

VIII Land and Sea

J.A. Steers (Professor of Geography at Cambridge), in his book *The Coastline of England and Wales* warns us against adopting too simple a view of coastal change. We hear from time to time about how many millimetres of Britain's coastline are consumed by the sea every year; we do not hear about the salt-marshes silting up. 'Accretion is far less spectacular than erosion . . . ' Yet far larger areas are gained each year by accretion than are lost by erosion, Professor Steers points out, citing a Royal Commission report of 1911: within a period of about thirty-five years 6,640 acres had been lost, and 48,000 acres gained. Interestingly the same *Mabinogion* tale of 'Branwen' which seemed to bear a memory of Britain and Ireland once having been only separated by a river illustrates this point about accretion. Brân and his followers sit on Harlech rock 'overlooking the sea'. That would have been the situation when the tale was written. The rock on which Harlech castle stands is now nearly a mile from the sea. This is a fairly recent change. In the 14th century Harlech was a port, and the castle could be reached by boat.

Similarly we are familiar with the sort of waves which batter our cliffs and tear away our beaches. We do not normally consider that it was another set of waves which in the first place put those beaches there.

It is clear from the geological record that there have been

enormous changes, but they have been changes both ways, and no linear pattern emerges, rather a continuous oscillation of rising and falling sea, accompanied, aggravated or counterparted by rising and falling land. There was a time (the 'carboniferous' period) when virtually the whole of England and Wales was under the sea, only Scotland remaining land. But that was hundreds of millions of years ago. The Ice Ages intervened, and brought very considerable changes in the relation of land and sea. These are comparatively easy to understand, but we have to bear in mind that there were at crucial times two sets of events taking place at the same time.

There were, it is thought, four advances and retreats of the ice-sheets. When the ice formed it locked up in glaciers and ice-caps a proportion of the amount of available water on earth. The effect of this was to make sea-levels everywhere drop. It has been estimated that at the peak of the ice formation sea-levels generally were four hundred feet lower than today. Land-bridges formed, between such places as Britain and the continent. Thus it is clear that several animal species reached Britain from the continent by land, but only a fraction of those present in continental Europe had made the journey before the melt replenished the sea and made us an island again. Britain has, for instance, only half as many indigenous mammals as Germany.

The pressure of the ice, however, also had a lowering effect on the land. Its weight caused continents and other land masses to sink. The result of this is that when the ice melts and the sea-level rises much goes under water.

The effects of melting are relatively fast. It is of course a self-accelerating process – a large amount of ice present keeps the air cool, and when there is less the temperature rises, making more ice melt. The last Ice Age ended fairly suddenly, in terms of geological time, about ten thousand years ago. The melting of the ice however had another effect, which complicates the general tendency for sea levels to rise in relation to land. The land which had been lowered by the weight of ice began to rise again. This rising is a process which is still going on. In cases such as that of the British Isles this means that while Scotland is going up, and has been for some time, the south coast of England is equivalently sinking. The island is tilting. This has had a noticeable effect during the last two thousand years. Steers refers to evidence of change in the sea levels of southern England since Roman times. Roman pottery has been found at Southwark indicating habitation five to six feet below present high water, which would not have occurred had this area then been subject to flooding. In parts of the Thames estuary the change in level since Roman times he estimates at some fifteen feet. At Tilbury Roman-British huts are about thirteen feet below high water, and the same subsidence is found at Southend. In the Thames-Medway the Roman occupation level is near low water. There low lying lands, once good grazing and now flooded, caused concern in medieval times, and banks were built in the 13th century, which had to be frequently raised. Villages have in some cases been damaged, such as Hallsands in Devon and Dunwick in Suffolk. The old church at Cromer in Norfolk had been washed by the sea for twenty years by 1337, and is now said to lie out at sea. The process continues. The London floods of January 6th-7th of 1928 are said to be the likely result of a gradual land subsidence. Since then of course there have been substantial flood-protection schemes.

In North Wales the changes since Roman times may be apparent from Tacitus' description of the way the army crossed the Menai Strait. It is evident that at least some of the horses walked across. In AD 61 when Suetonius invaded the island he used flat-bottomed boats 'to contend with the shifting shallows' to ferry over the infantry; but some of the cavalry 'utilized fords'. Some seventeen years later when Agricola completed the conquest of Anglesey he chose men 'who had experience of fords', as well as some who could swim with their horses beside them, thus surprising the enemy, who had been expecting a fleet.

It is thought likely that at least during the early stages of the rising of sections of the earth's crust which had been pressed down by billions of tons of ice there would be a high incidence of earthquakes. Graham Hancock speculates, in the book already referred to, that in view of this and the flooding of populated areas by the fast-melting ice, myths of cataclysm could be 'accurate eye-witness accounts' of conditions experienced at the end of the last Ice Age. He puts the period of catastrophes as being between 15,000 and 8,000 BC We are reminded of the time given in Plato's account of the flourishing of Atlantis, as being seven thousand years before the time of Solon, a date often dismissed as error, which should perhaps be more seriously considered.

It is strange but significant that the best scientific opinion concerning Llys Helig accords with this supposition of Hancock's. Both Steers and North, as part of their programme of discrediting the legend, give the view that though there was at one time dry land in the area of Llys Helig, it was (says Steers) 'before the close of the post-Glacial period', which coincided with 'the last downward movement of the coast'. Geological and archaeological evidence, according to North, show a change in sea level from about 8000 BC, and thus during Neolithic times. This approximate time is attested by such evidence as there is elsewhere. In 1988 a Neolithic village, said to be about 8000 years old, was found underwater off the coast of Israel. It had lain in a small valley, and the sea had broken through a sandstone ridge. The process of sea-level change is so well-established that it has been given a name: 'eustatic', meaning 'denoting or relating to world-wide changes in sea level caused by melting of ice sheets, movements of ocean floors, sedimentation, etc.'

Steers is briefly dismissive of the legend of Llys Helig, hardly surprisingly since his source and authority is North, whose arguments he accepts without question. Written originally in the 1940's, even his 1964 revised edition cannot bring him up to date, since in it he laments the lack of an aerial photograph, which he thinks would prove North's point that the stones at Llys Helig do not form a regular structure. For him it is a natural glacial deposit, 'the remains of a moraine eroded away by the waves'. The story, like that of Cantre'r Gwaelod, 'may have been introduced' to this site. Folk tales have been handed down possibly from Neolithic times, 'and in course of time have been made to apply to specific objects popularly supposed to be of human construction'. It is true that at one time 'Wales certainly extended farther seawards, and moraines would be scattered on this now submerged surface: their erosion would produce just such features as those of Llys Helig to-day'.

Steers spends a bit more time on Cantre'r Gwaelod, and in particular the nature of the 'sarns', those long straight stretches of stone which run out at right-angles to the coast into Cardigan Bay.

He deals with five 'causeways' of differing lengths. He tells the Cantre'r Gwaelod story, but dismisses any connection to it of the causeways: the sarns are natural.

Nevertheless he acknowledges the evidence of submerged forests, for instance at Borth, which point to considerable subsidence. 'Are there,' he asks, 'any means . . . of correlating folklore and physiography?' Rather surprisingly, given his otherwise aloof scientific attitude to story, he considers the possibility that the characteristic attributes of folk-tale lake-dwellers – a fear or iron, dislike of the plough, and so on – relate them to early inhabitants of Wales, giving rise to the idea that the tales 'go back at least as far as the first contacts of the iron-users with the earlier inhabitants of Wales' and others even to the first contact of Bronze Age people with their Neolithic predecessors. Evidence that very early settlements occurred at the edges of lakes is abundant throughout Britain, and this position would of course make them vulnerable to changes in water level. In Neolithic times the boulder clay reached far out into Cardigan Bay, and the present river system wound through it to mouths far seaward of the present coast. Post-glacial submergence included the Neolithic period, but there is no reason to think that it continued after it. So Steers opines.

Steers reveals again his dependence on North, though this time without acknowledgement, by venturing into a further area of speculation. In 1916 H.K. Fleure and T.C. James published in the *Journal of the Royal Anthropological Institute* a paper entitled 'Geographical Distribution of Anthropological Types in Wales', in which they showed, by comparison of skull measurements, that many people still living in Wales then, particularly in remoter areas, were descended from the Neolithic inhabitants. This could of course be done now with much greater certainty by DNA analysis, and no doubt it will be, if it has not been done already without my knowledge. My point here is simply that Steers, and before him North, believed it, and drew the following conclusions: Neolithic people could have been living on the boulder-clay lands which are now below the sea at the time of their submergence; perhaps (as North says in *Sunken Cities*) 'what they witnessed was slow encroachment due to a series of minor inundations, not a single wide-spread catastrophe' – but of course perhaps not: and, as Steers now says, it is quite possible that the present, or rather the 1916 Neolithic descendants' ancestors 'should have witnessed the submergence of these boulder-clay lands'. 'In brief,' writes Steers, 'it would be quite unjustifiable to dismiss these legends as mere nonsense in their entirety.'

The idea of this source of origin for the stories is not new. Sir John Lloyd, for instance, in his *History of Wales*, in 1939, wonders whether perhaps

> . . . in the well-known Cantref y Gwaelod and Traeth Lafan legends, which are stories of the submergence of flourishing realms beneath the pitiless sea, we may not have reminiscences, handed down through many generations of the effects, at times, perhaps, startling, of the gradual subsidence of the coastal margins.

North points out as well that elsewhere, for instance on the east coast of England, Neolithic and Bronze Age people were abandoning their coastal sites in the face of rising sea levels. This was, he says, 'a slowly progressive menace, not a sudden overwhelming catastrophe'.

This is not necessarily true, since there have been, and still are, sudden catastrophic inundations around our coasts and rivers, the effects of which could become permanent if it were not for human intervention. Giraldus Cambrensis, in the 1180's, mentions a storm of 1171-2, in St Bride's Bay,

Newgale, South Wales, when 'by the extraordinary violence of a storm, the surface of the earth, which had been covered for many ages, reappeared, and discovered the trunks of trees cut off, standing in the very sea itself . . . ' North, in *Sunken Cities*, cites depictions of the great Severn estuary flood of 1607, in which people are shown as having climbed to the tops of trees, just as in Ovid's description of Deucalion's flood (which perhaps influenced the illustrator), as being a possible influence on the writer of *Notes to be Observed* . . . ; and Steers himself is much impressed by the effect on our attention to the matter of the great storm-surge of 1953. In our own time we have become familiar with the concept of 'flash floods', and it is of particular significance to us here, I think, in this investigation, that after the inundation of much of the British midlands in the autumn of the year 2000, the Prince of Wales admonished the leaders of British industry with the accusation that the cause of this was human greed and arrogance – so perpetuating an ancient tradition, as we now know, of seeing natural disaster as being the outcome of human transgression, visited on our sinful heads now by our new (though no less angry) deities, the global forces.

We saw in the last chapter that according to Dr Ballard the breaking through of the waters of the rising Mediterranean to submerge the area which is now the Black Sea would have been a quite sudden event, and more recently it has been claimed that the effects of gradually rising sea levels at the end of the Ice Age were accelerated by the incidence of a *tsunami*, a giant tidal wave forty foot high. Professor David Smith, professor of geography at Coventry University, told the British Association for the Advancement of Science's Festival, meeting at Glasgow in September 2001, that evidence had been discovered (in the form of datable sand deposits along the coast of Scotland) that in about 5800 BC a vast underwater landslide off the coast of Stavanger in Norway caused such a wave to inundate suddenly much of the landbridge that then connected Britain to the continent, at a time when rising sea levels were carrying out the process of isolating us gradually. 'It would,' he said, 'have been a devastating event for people living there.' There is, at the same time, speculation that a *tsunami* effect could take place again: if, or when, the volcano Cumbre Viejo on the Canary island of La Palma erupts and casts its side into the sea a wave again forty foot high will travel a mile inland in southwest England obliterating everything in its path. Moreover its effects will be greater when they reach the other side of the Atlantic, and cities such as New York and Miami will be virtually obliterated, an area up to six miles inland inundated. This, however, said its proponent, Dr Simon Day of the Hazard Research Centre at University College London, is 'unlikely to happen in the next century'.

That there was dry land once in Conwy Bay, and elsewhere on the North Wales coast where the sea now is, is not disputed, nor could it be since the most immediate form of empirical evidence is available: you can see the evidence for it for yourself. Writer after writer on the subject of Llys Helig refers to the tree-stumps, the still remaining evidence of a submerged forest. The writer of the *Notes to be Observed* was quoted on the subject in Chapter II, which passage it will be convenient to repeat here:

In this great wash uppon a lowe ebbe, in every March and June

(corrected to 'August')

are to be seen the rootes of greate oake and ashe att the furthest ebbe att all but onely uppon spring tydes in March and August; this I speake as an eye wittnes, havynge seene the rootes my sealf and taken them upp, soe that ytt shoulde seeme that this vale before the inundacion was a woodland countrey.

That was written some time between 1621 and 1625. In the 18th century Thomas Pennant made similar remarks about the coast off Abergele:

The small town of *Abergeleu* lies about a mile from *Cefn Ogo* near the clayey cliffs which impend over the sea. Tradition says, that in old times that element had overwhelmed a vast tract of inhabited country once extending at least two miles northward;

He then mentions a grave-stone set in the church-yard wall which claims to commemorate a man who lived three miles to the north of it; but since as he says this bears no date, and might indeed have come from anywhere (since it does not appear to relate to a local grave) we need not discuss this further.

But, as a better proof, I have observed, at low-water, far from the clayey banks, a long tract of hard loam filled with the bodies of oak trees, tolerably entire; but so soft as to be cut with a knife as easily as wax.
   The wood is collected by the poorer people, and, after being brought to dry upon the beach, is carried home and used as fuel; but, in burning, it emits a very bad smell.

113

If indeed these ancient trunks were used as firewood, it is amazing that there are any of them left. When William Ashton came to an adjoining area in 1908 he found fewer than apparently Pennant did.

> Ancient forest remains are again encountered on the beach south of Rhos pier. The writer found only a small number of stumps on his visit here in 1908, but in October, 1917, he saw, opposite the point where the tramroad turns inland several stumps *in situ* and still more prostrate . . . As at most other points, there is a lower arboreal bed. Tree trunks could also be well seen within the last 30 or 40 years on the beach opposite Old Colwyn railway station.

In September 1909, the *Llandudno Advertiser* announced a discovery ('Interesting Discovery in Conway Bay') which resulted from a set of perhaps unique conditions. The North Deep channel had moved to nearer the West Shore, and thousands of tons of sand appeared to have been carried away; an unusually low tide allowed Mr John Roberts, of Bryn Celyn, the sight of trees embedded there in red clay, 'about 200 yards to the s.w. from the Toll House'. They were well rooted there, and he traced one root a length of about twenty feet. In addition, and quite close to high water, were the remains of a gigantic tree, which he judged to have been an oak. A second visit some weeks later, with other interested people, confirmed all this. The shore, he said, had not 'been in this state within the memory of anyone now living, probably centuries have passed since it bore a similar appearance'. However 'It is to be feared' (the Advertiser says of the second visit) 'that the remains will not be visible very much longer, for there are already indications that the sand is being gradually driven back, and a few more tides, especially should there be some strong westerly gales, may see the remains covered for a few more generations'. The *Advertiser* continues:

> This discovery is of great importance as forming another link in the chain of evidence connecting what is now known as Conway Bay with Cantref Gwalod, (*sic*) which has been described as a 'most delicate vale, abounding in fruitfulness and excelling all other vales in fertility and plentifulness'.

Steers says that submerged forests 'seem to imply a fairly rapid submergence'. He mentions many around the coast of Britain, and quite a number in North Wales: near Cricieth; at Llanaber; between Borth and Ynyslas. He devotes a section of a chapter to the knowledge gained of these and their associated peat beds by pollen analysis. He says of them in general that they 'are often closely associated with former land surfaces which sometimes contain the remains of ancient man, and more often those of his artefacts'.

This topic was the subject of two papers by J. Reid Moir published in the *Journal of the Royal Anthropological Institute* in 1921 and 1925 giving details of a very large number of flints found in the forest beds off the coast of Cromer, where at low tides and after scouring the remains of trees could be seen, and along with some mammalian remains the evidence of a complete flint workshop.

There is nothing so effective as touching it to convince yourself of a thing's existence. The tree-stumps are undoubtedly made of wood – not fossilised or petrified, but sea-saturated, grain-ribbed wood. They remain very firmly rooted where they grew. Presumably if they ever dried out they would crumble away to dust, but being exposed only at low tide they never stand this test. The ones I looked at on the beach at Conwy Morfa are about two metres below present high water. There are several stumps relatively close together, the roots of other trees which have disappeared, and one complete recumbent trunk with branches, lying in the clay. All around, one begins to see, is the debris of afforestation, twigs and branches, even, I am told, under the clay, complete leaves preserved intact by the sealing effect of the clay, which decay rapidly once exposed. My informant, Nigel Bannerman, described the ground here as 'forest floor litter'. The trees, he thinks in this case, were probably Scots pine.

These trees, he pointed out, are evidence not only of the one-time extent of dry land; they testify too to several very extensive changes in the relation of land to sea. They are rooted in blue clay, which Nigel says is estuarine in origin, and was therefore laid down when the sea level was roughly as it is now. The sea then retreated, for sufficient time for a forest to become established on its former shore. It rose again, and the trees died. You get assailed on that beach by contrary forces: the undeniability and the sheer improbability of that ebb and flow.

In December 1995, two samples of submerged tree-stumps were sent by Bangor University for carbon dating, one from Llanddwyn Island, Anglesey, another from the North Shore at Llandudno. Some of those behind the enterprise were secretly hoping that the samples would produce Dark Age dates, and thus validate the legend of Llys Helig. They were to be disappointed. Give or take 90 years, the Anglesey sample was dated at 6925 years Before Present. The Llandudno sample (where the stumps lie low down on the Lower Peat beds, laid down about eight thousand years ago) gave a date, plus or minus 45 years, of 6985. It is thus scientifically established that these trees grew nearly seven thousand years ago. The ones at Conwy, being higher on the shore, are perhaps some thousand years or so younger.

That this particular coast is subject to fairly fast erosion is shown by the case of Castell Tremlyd, at one time a large earthwork on the point between Deganwy and Llandudno locally known as Black Rocks. Lewis Morris' charts of the early 18th century show it clearly, lying to seaward of the present point. A map of about 1820 identifies the spot, but says in brackets 'no visible trace remaining'. On the 1830 Admiralty charts this has become known as 'Tremlyd Pt.', and in the 1849 guidebook to Llandudno 'Castell Tremlydd' appears to have become the name of a farm some way inland.

It is hardly surprising that much work has been, and is at present being done, on the matter of coastal erosion. In the spring of 2001 a study found that a two hundred yard stretch of dunes in Meirionnydd was being whittled away by the sea at the rate of several yards a year, threatening the loss of thousands of acres of farmland in the Artro valley and serious flooding in Llanbedr village. The Little Orme at Penrhyn Bay was noted, in an Internet report, to be crumbling away into the sea; Colwyn Bay promenade, often closed to traffic in stormy conditions, had part of the roadway washed away; loss of sand-dunes due to coastal drift threatened further serious problems. Sea defence schemes were found to be necessary at Llandudno, Towyn and Kinmel Bay as well as at Rhos-on-Sea. These are just local examples, and no doubt studies all around our coast have produced comparable results.

In a paper titled 'Tidal Aggression', published in *The*

Seafarer in the summer edition of 2001, Gordon McDonald achieves an overview of the situation. As a result of investigation of the Severn estuary (where invasions of South Wales have left remains of ancient ports) McDonald concluded that the fact that sea level was not constant made it 'one of the most accurate barometers of long-term global climatic variation'. He found 'with astonishment and initially disbelief' that the cycles of sea-level rise and fall formed a regular pattern, with each cycle taking a thousand years to complete. 'What was even more astonishing was the fact that the peaks and troughs during each cycle were far more acute than anyone could have predicted.' Between 300BC and 80 AD sea level, he found, rose by almost six metres. The matter is far from being a simple movement. After 80 AD it began a steady fall, rising again in the eighth and ninth centuries to peak at about 1100 AD, since when it had been falling again until recently.

McDonald points to the relatively fast changes in climate which have taken place during this period, information now available to us through the science of dendrochronology as well as chronicled records. A long period of gradual warming peaked about 1225 but continued to the end of the 13th century. In the 14th century the climate deteriorated so much that river flooding made winter travel difficult. In Monmouth, for instance, it is recorded that in 1349 it rained every day from July to Christmas, causing people to abandon their houses in the river sector of the town. Not much, we feel, looking at footage of the flooded streets of 2000, has changed.

Yet it did change, and quite dramatically, in between. By the end of the 15th century the fall of sea level had exposed the course of ancient rivers and the remains of early settlements along the south coast, settlements lost in rising tides of the ninth and tenth centuries. The fall in sea level correlates with a pattern of world cooling, intermittently during the 15th century and the last quarter of the 16th, reaching the period known as the 'Little Ice Age' in the 17th, when the previous pattern of dry summers was reversed.

It is hardly surprising that, with this knowledge behind him, McDonald does not pay much heed to the claims that global warming is being caused, or exacerbated, by human activity. 'The surface climate of the earth is influenced by a huge variety of elements of which volcanic activity, cosmic storms on the sun and unpredictable seasonal variations are but a few to mention.' He says that the common theme with all predictions of global warming is a 'general lack of understanding of long term climate change' together with preconceived assumptions, which has led to 'a plethora of conflicting reports with dire predictions of exaggerated changes in sea level'. Our climate in Britain has (in its present cycle) been getting warmer since the 17th century, 'and concurrent with this is a slow but progressive rise in sea level'. As far as the future is concerned, he thinks that (on the basis of past trends) both global warming and rising sea level will stabilise during the last decades of this century.

Here we are not concerned with the future but with the past, so that this is not the place to discuss the question of the possible effect on global warming, and tide-levels, of the emission of 'greenhouse gases'. The past has shown us that purely natural causes (such as took place long before we were around, let alone industrialised) are sufficient, without our help, to cause vast and devastating change. One such change, perhaps one in an infinite cycle, caused the submergence of fertile lands in Conwy Bay, some seven thousand years ago.

The datable tree-stumps prove it. This is as hard a fact as

one can get. Moreover evidence from other similar sites shows that there were people here, amongst these trees. If a piece of trunk can remain rooted in this place for so long a time, and be here now for me to touch it, so too could something much less destructible, because less material – the memory of the land they lost.

You think it improbable that information could be transmitted over so long a time. But consider: if you were told something by your grand-parents which you then told to your grand-children, you would have caused the transfer of information over perhaps a hundred and fifty years. Thus it takes only the lifetimes of twenty people to span three thousand years. We may recall here the references in the myths to five generations.

North mentions, in *Sunken Cities*, 'the numerous stories of old people who could remember living or reaping on sites now covered by the sea, or whose parents had recollections of so doing'. I remember that when I was a child living on the western shore of the Great Orme the two large upright rocks on the beach at the bottom of our garden were the subject of such a story. We were told that there was (or had been) an old man living in the town who remembered his grandfather saying that he used to plough around those rocks. It is always, it seems, somebody's grandfather, who remembers such things.

Formalised and stylised by time, like a beach stone rounded by millennia of motion, the story of a memory takes a shape which facilitates the process of remembering and transmitting it, thus reinforcing its own durability. The core of the record, so preserved, gets passed to us in a still recognisable form.

This is not the whole explanation of Llys Helig. Nobody would suggest that what we have here are the ruins of a stone-built palace dating from about 7000 BC. Nevertheless whatever one thinks of the story and its possible origins, of its validity or otherwise as myth, as North puts it 'the stones themselves still remain' – and require some sort of interpretation.

IX   Antiquarians in Boats

St Seiriol built himself a pavement to walk dryshod from his church at Priestholm (now, since the 'greate and lamentable inundacion', the island known as Puffin Island and *Ynys Seiriol*) to his chapel at Penmaenmawr. An interesting additional piece of information is the reason for the construction of this causeway: ' . . . the vale beynge very lowe grownd and wette', indicating that even if the final inundation was sudden it may have been heralded by an increasing rise in water level.

The author of *Notes to be Observed* (to whom we owe the above record), he who had seen the submerged tree-stumps himself and 'taken them upp', had evidently inspected that pavement too: ' . . . which pavemt may att this day bee discerned from Penmen Mawr to Priestholme when the sea is cleere, yf a man liste to goe in a bote to see ytt.'

That, we know, was in the first half of the 1620's. For a hundred years or so people had by then become increasingly interested in studying the past at first hand. John Leland, for example, came through Wales in the 1530's, noting antiquities, and he remarked on the story of the lost lands of Cardigan Bay, which the 'se ful many a yere syns hath clene devour'd'. He does not, North points out, mention the other story in Conwy Bay.

Although the author of the *Notes* is often quoted as our first direct observer, the first to make the physical connection of the Llys Helig legend with the group of rocks, and although he did undoubtedly see for himself the tree-stumps and probably Seiriol's causeway, there is no evidence in the text to indicate that he actually saw the supposed Llys itself, 'the ruynes whereof is now to bee seene uppon a grownd ebbe some two myles within the sea directly over against Trevyn yr Wylva'. He does not describe the ruins at all, and at that point changes the subject to recount the aftermath of the inundation. More detail is given in a book by a schoolmaster called William Williams, a *History of Beaumaris* written in 1669, which is now lost but was fortunately quoted by Richard Fenton in his *Tours of Wales* in the early 19th century: The story of Helig

> gains the more credit because there are ruins of old Walls to be seen in that place to this very day at Equinoctial tides. And because wrought and carved free Stones and Iron bars of Windows and other Irons belonging to buildings have been found there. And the Compiler of this history hath been told by antient people of Ty Mawr (now the Mansion House of Robert Coytmore Esq. not far distant) that they had seen Iron bars of Windows and other Irons come from thence.

The rocks appear to have been named as a 'Llys' for the first time by the chart-maker Lewis Morris, who produced a chart of Conwy Bay in 1748, and although he mistakenly calls the site 'Llys Elis ap Clynnog' he undoubtedly knew the rocks as a reality. Indeed it is probable that they featured in their physical form more prominently in the field of navigation, as landmark or hazard, than they did on land. In his notes *Celtic Remains* Morris says somewhat doubtfully that the Llys had been 'overwhelmed by the sea, as tradition has it, and buildings are pretended to have been seen under water', and in the text accompanying the 1801 publication of his Irish Sea charts it is remarked (perhaps by his son William, who produced the edition) 'A buoy is much wanted on that patch of foul ground, called Llys Ellis ap Clynog'.

Morris' identification of the spot set the standard for later map-makers, and four years later William Owen reproduced it (though placing the rocks rather further off shore) in his engraving for Warrington's *History of Wales*. Now it is correctly named as Llys Helig ab Glanog, and underneath the name Owen wrote 'overflowed in the 6th cent'y'. The first Ordnance Survey map of the area, published in 1841, marks and names the stones, but appears to place them half a mile or so too far east.

It is ironic but unsurprising that the first recorded trip apparently in search of the stones failed to find them, though, like the author of the *Notes*, the explorer had no trouble locating the supposed causeway. Edward Pugh, a painter and topographical writer born at Ruthin in 1761, produced a book in 1812 called *Cambria Depicta*, recording years of travel on foot in the North Wales area bounded by Chester and Shrewsbury. He took a boat and boatman out from Puffin Island, and

> we floated over the place where tradition says one Helig Voel ab Glanog, a chieftain of the sixth century, had great possessions, extending far into the bay; but which were suddenly overwhelmed by the sea. It is said that at very low ebbs, ruined houses are yet to be seen, and a causeway pointing from Priestholme-island to Penmaenmawr. This causeway, indeed, is easily visible; the boatman placing me right over it, and keeping the boat's head to the tide; enabled me to examine it well . . . From the certainty of the existence

of this causeway, we may venture to give credit to the existence of the remains of Helig's houses . . .

A Llandudno boatman called Huw Roberts made the trip about 1844, but we do not know who, if anyone, went with him, and the results were never published. He it was, however, who took the members of the first fully recorded trip to carry out any sort of detailed investigation of the stones. They went the long way, setting off from Llandudno's north shore at 2 p.m., 19th August, 1864, and first rowing around the Great Orme. They had with them the Lewis Morris chart, and they knew of the legend as recorded in the version of *Notes to be Observed* published in the *Cambrian Quarterly Magazine* in 1831.

Charlton Hall, the party's leader, was accompanied by two clergymen, as well as the boatman and his son. One of the passengers was the Reverend Richard Parry, Llandudno's Welsh Congregational Minister, also known by his Bardic name of 'Gwalchmai' – but North gives the name at one point, presumably in error, as 'The Rev. B. Parry'. Richard Parry it was, in any case, who first wrote up the account, which was published in Welsh in *Baner ac Amserau Cymru* on 21st September, 1864, in other words quite soon after the trip. The other passenger was also a clergyman, the Reverend Thomas F. Fergie, incumbent of Ince, Wigan. It is not known whether he published any record of the trip.

Charlton Hall himself is variously described. Ashton says he was 'a Liverpool gentleman', with which North agrees; and it was to the Liverpool Geological Society that he reported his findings, in a paper given on 13th December, 1864, published in their 'Proceedings' for 1864/5. Tom Parry refers to him as 'a local geologist', but as he was apparently a wine-merchant his interest in geology might have been a hobby. His paper (generally rather pompous, and consistently weakly reasoned) shows some ignorance of glacial features, recognised in geological circles since the 1840's.

They searched the seas offshore from Trwyn yr Wylfa, for a long time in vain. Hall, steering, put the boat out to sea, keeping the mark of Trwyn yr Wylfa at their back.

The fact was, we had been searching too close inland. We had not run out to seaward long when the boatmen called our attention to a black mass upon the surface of the water, and over which it was breaking. We made all speed, and quickly came up to the object of our search. All we could see, however, was sea weed running in regular lines. Running up into and alongside the sea weed I found, by taking off my coat and stripping my arms, that the weed grew upon the top of what appeared to have been a wall. I pulled up some of the stones; some were too large to be dislodged, but by pulling slowly along the line of weed it became evident that the stones ran in straight lines, and, so far as could be judged by feeling, they appeared to be just as the stones of a wall would be after being thrown down by the action of the sea, until those on either side would support the rest . . .

Hall thought he could detect a central area in which there were no stones, and interpreted this as a courtyard or the inside of a large apartment. Several of them set about drawing plans, using the seaweed as a guide to where the stones were, all of which, according to Richard Parry, turned out remarkably similar. They did not, Hall and Parry both admit, take measurements, either of the dimensions of the 'walls' or of the angles. They assumed deeper water in the middle, where they could see no sign of stones, but even so Parry evidently thought he had found signs of a circular round tower in the middle. Charlton Hall concluded that they had found

> . . . evidence of the truth of the legend that there, on that spot – now covered by the sea, and at least two miles out from the nearest land – did once stand a grand old hall of magnificent dimensions, of whose shape and proportions there still remain distinguishable traces.

They did not have long to do all this, and as we shall see it is one of Llys Helig's alluring characteristics that no-one ever does. Low water was at 5 p.m. Soon after that the stones were submerged again. The weather was worsening, and they were glad to beach on the West Shore at nine in the evening.

Nothing more came of this, beyond the continuing existence of the sketch-maps and the two reports. Interest in Llys Helig is sporadic, and nobody seems to have wanted to visit it again for more than forty years. It was at the beginning of the twentieth century that the spate of inspections started which in effect forms the present series. W. Bezant Lowe had published in 1906 an edition of the *Notes to be Observed*, and in September 1907 he decided to go and try to observe for himself. He set out with Mr W.J.P. Arrowsmith of Deganwy, but they did not have much luck. Conditions are so critical for the viewing of Llys Helig that it is amazing that anyone has ever seen it. Even a slight onshore breeze can make the waves break over the stones, preventing a proper view of them. Maybe this is what obstructed Lowe and Arrowsmith. We know that they got there, but were unable to make a proper inspection, and the trip produced no official report.

Ashton was very much luckier, on 13th September the next year. Not only was there then an unusually low tide, but conditions generally were 'highly favourable'. He set off at dawn from the Penmaenmawr coast, which involved hauling a boat, in company with its owner, local boatman Richard Thomas, across three or four hundred yards of soft sand, before they could launch.

Local boatmen, says Ashton (and he had one with him) knew the place as rocky ground, and best avoided at low tide. They found it by its trademark of black seaweed, and reached it on cue at low tide. Ashton stood on a projecting boulder and viewed the area. He saw three sides of a large square, 'with a large rectangular recess at the south-west side', consisting of straight lines of wall.

> These stones did not vary six inches from a straight line. They seemed to form the apex of a base of thrown-down stones, forming protecting supports, which would account for the walls enduring through so many centuries. One could not confidently say that the stones had ever been masoned, nor that they had been mortared together, though they may have been so.

He measured the wall on the Deganwy side as 130 yards. It had a large stone standing up in it, and another large one lay beneath the water, 'as if they had formed two pillars of a gateway'. He found a causeway of stones connecting these two with the eastern corner, and heading out towards Penmaenbach. He failed to find a wall on the north side, open to the sea, and concluded that the waves had demolished it. Then comes the conclusion which we mentioned at the start of this book: 'It is quite impossible for anyone to view these 350 or more yards of strictly rectangular remains and to entertain the slightest doubt as to their having been human handiwork.'

He does not, however, fully endorse Charlton Hall's vision of a grand old hall. There are, he says, 'strong reasons for the belief that these are not the walls of any actual building. They more probably formed the boundaries of a courtyard surrounding Helig's abode, the purpose of the walls being for defence against attack or for the herding of cattle, or for both purposes. No early Welsh castles, prior to about the 13th century, were built of stone'.

Ashton usefully pinpoints Llys Helig's position: it lies 'about 1½ miles N. by N.W. of Penmaenmawr Station, and lies on a line connecting Beaumaris with Deganwy'.

Six months after the Ashton trip the Llandudno and District Field Club set out for the rocks, on 23rd March, 1909, led by G.A. Humphreys. They had the assistance of boatman John Roberts, who, as a boy, had been there with Charlton Hall in 1864. This time they had the sense to send the boat round the Orme in advance, and embarked from near the Gogarth Abbey Hotel at 4 p.m. They had arranged to meet Bezant Lowe on the site, he approaching from the Penmaenmawr side.

The weather was calm but visibility conditions were poor: 'it was too misty to see the Great Orme to take any bearings and the water was muddy'. On the way out they examined any stones showing above water. A ridge of stones revealed two lengths higher than the rest, which they inspected carefully. Some large stones on top were removed, exposing to view 'stones placed one on top of the other in such a way as to give the impression that it was the work of human hands . . . ' They landed on an island of stones, and inspected some unusually flat ones. Removing some loose ones 'there was exhibited a good characteristic specimen of the lowest part of what I may term rough walling . . . ' While they were engaged in this inspection 'two other boats came down from Deganwy and went on westwards to "Llys Helig"'. It turns out that Humphreys and his party did not get to Llys Helig at all: 'I considered the ridges and flat stones referred to of sufficient interest to warrant watching same down to the time of dead low water and therefore it was too late to row the extra mile westward to meet Mr Lowe at Llys Helig.' It seems they ended up examining some other rocks, about a mile south-east of the site, which they thought might be part of the causeway linking Llys Helig to Penmaenbach. Once again they concluded that 'human hands had laid the stones'. According to Ashton and Tom Parry what they had examined were the boulders known as the Burlingham Rocks. They came home with difficulty in the dark, after what Humphreys calls in his Memorandum 'quite an adventurous trip'.

It seems that this cannot have been the same Field Club trip of 1909 as that reported by North in his paper, when he says 'the site was again visited' by members of the Club including L.S. Underwood and R.J. Gresley Jones, who are not mentioned by Humphreys. Underwood told North 'that the stones had the appearance not of actual walls but of walls that had been thrown down and the stones scattered on either side'. North clearly understood him to be speaking of Llys Helig. 'He expressed the opinion that "the whole of the site appeared to be more artificial than natural".' We thus have an implication of a second trip, for which I do not know of any report. In 1939 Gresley Jones writes in the

Weekly News of 'my inspection of the site 30 years ago', though the same article says that he and Underwood 'were members of the 1913 expedition'.

Luck definitely forms one of the factors governing these trips. Llys Helig plays a guessing game with us, the rules of which are stringent – the incidence of those rare and early morning tides – but the moves controlled by the random dice of wind and weather. You need calm water, and clear sea. The initial crucial and governing factors combined with the element of chance perhaps explain the thirty and forty year gaps, between these bouts of expeditions. You get, realistically, three chances a year. Since the two of maximum low tides occur equinoctially, in March and September, when high winds are also prevalent, the August one would seem to be the most favourable, and that most likely to take place in a good light. In March and September you are waiting for the dawn, or coming home in the dusk.

Bezant Lowe and the Field Club both threw losing moves. Luck however was with the next explorer, Mr Horace Lees, a resident of Deganwy, who went on 3rd September, 1913, setting off from anchorage at Deganwy at 5.20 a.m. He for the first time managed to photograph the site, showing its snaking lines, which he took to be wall foundations.

> The west wall ran almost north and south for some 70 yards above sea level, and a further 20 or 30 yard to the north below the sea. Between the two pieces there appeared to have been a gateway. At the south extremity the wall turned abruptly at a right angle to the east, running quite straight for 100 or 120 yards.

Although Lees clearly saw what he had hoped to see, Helig's palace, he had to admit that the walls showed no sign of mortar, and 'little trace of shaping or squaring on any of the stones examined'. Writing of his investigation in *The Field*, for 4th October, 1913, he announces the conclusion that the walls themselves 'served only to enclose a courtyard where cattle could be driven in times of stress. It is on the great bank that the palace must have stood, and any relics will be buried here beneath the stones'. The use of right-angles, however, led Lees to dismiss the early-British date and go instead for a Roman one. Lees drew an apparently accurate plan, which Ashton reproduces with his own addition of the east wall.

Although there follows one of those remarkable gaps as far as recorded trips to Llys Helig are concerned, from 1913 to 1939, it seems likely that people continued to go there in between. 'Members of Llandudno, Colwyn Bay and District Field Club,' writes its Chairman. G.A. Humphreys, in his Foreword to North's paper, 'have made many excursions to the alleged site of "Llys Helig" and varying views have been expressed in regard to what was seen.' What happened to set off the 1939 trip, with all its consequences, actually took place a few years earlier. We mentioned North's talk to the Field Club at the start of Chapter II, and his disclaimer of any intention to debunk the popular local legend. His suggestions, he said, were merely to the effect that much supposed evidence for the connection of the legend with the site was invalid, and such valid evidence as there was showed that the stones could not have been part of human habitations at the times the legend referred to. 'These suggestions were, naturally, not acceptable to those who had come to regard the story as history . . . ', some of whom had actually visited the site, which North had not. In fact, as Tom Parry expresses it, the suggestion 'caused much consternation amongst members . . . ' They challenged North to go to see for himself, and he accepted. However the trip had to wait a further three years, and it was not until 17th August, 1939 that it took place. The party consisted largely of believers; North and Grimes, the archaeological expert, being the only sceptics.

Humphreys himself could not go, as he had a bad cold. Underwood and Gresley Jones were, the *North Wales Weekly News* informs us, 'the only two members of a former expedition', providing possible evidence of a trip which seems to be unrecorded. Dr Willoughby Gardner and two other members of the committee added to the distinguished passenger list, and a Mr L. Munroe of H.M. Office of Works, and Mr H.E. Brothers, B.Sc., provided further expertise. It was quite an event, and earned extensive media coverage.

The met on Deganwy beach at 4 a.m. The main party embarked on the Lark, a boat owned by Councillor Nick Parkinson. A second boat carried photographers and press. There was mist on the sea, the Orme showing above it, as the sun came up. The *North Wales Weekly News*, whose editor, Asa Davies was in the Lark, carried a full report on 24th August.

The stones appeared about half-past six. The seaweed first, then the black heads of rocks. Grimes put on a bathing suit and, wading, actually collected samples of rocks from all around the site. His verdict was later to become the most adamant. 'As a result of what I saw with my eyes and felt with my hands – and feet – I have felt obliged to decide that whatever else it might be, this collection of stones was *not* the remains of an ancient building or of any other ancient structure.'

The expedition had been prepared to see walls. They even intended to carry out a survey, under the direction of Willoughby Gardner. Grimes concedes that at first sight 'the dark, narrow lines which appeared on the surface of the water had every appearance of walls'. North later showed, using a sheet of paper, how a roughly curved shape could take on such an appearance, when viewed along its plane at near eye level. 'It soon became clear,' Grimes reports, 'that the distant appearance was deceptive.' The so-called lines, which look narrow and wall-like from a boat, are in fact not narrow banks or ridges at all, but consist of stones which 'extend over a wide area the limits of which I did not succeed in defining in any direction'. The site does not consist, he said, of a series of ridges, but 'of an apparently unbroken mass of boulders which in some places were banked up higher than in others'. His main argument against these having been walls was that the stones 'are of a type not suited for building purposes'. They are smooth and round, irregular in shape, and of varying sizes. 'I saw no sign of any shaping or dressing.' However it must be pointed out that all this could be said of many field and mountain walls in North Wales. Grimes acknowledges this, but points out that in the case of such walls the larger stones would predominate at the base, and remain there when the wall collapsed. 'At Llys Helig there was no sign of this. The large stones were scattered all over the area . . . and other smaller stones are inextricably mixed with them.' North confirms the view that the stones are of all shapes and sizes, 'from masses weighing tons down to rounded pieces comparable in size to eggs and marbles. No walls could have been built with such a heterogeneous assemblage . . . '. The extensive spread of the stones would, if they were the remains of walls, have implied (says Grimes) 'structures so high that they could not possibly have remained stable in view of the unsatisfactory character of the material from which they would have been built'. He thought the trip had been worthwhile, for the light it threw on the submerged land surface and coastal change. 'A romantic legend and the stones remains for those who prefer it so.'

Tom Parry draws attention to an oddity associated with this trip which has never been explained. North said in his report 'No air photograph, unfortunately, has been taken to show the real plan of the site . . . '. Yet apparently an aircraft was supposed to have flown over the site that morning, but failed to arrive. It did however fly over in the evening, but the R.A.F. pilot who carefully inspected the site does not seem to have reported his conclusions, and for some reason, the *Weekly News* tells us, he 'did not take photographs'.

A Press Conference took place that evening in the Deganwy Castle Hotel. The *Weekly News* reports:

> Mr Grimes opened with the definite statement that nothing he had seen or found indicated that the site was of archaeological importance.

The *Llandudno Advertiser* reports on 26th August: Mr Gresley Jones accepted Grimes' finding of a lack of evidence of the remains of a structure, 'but he does challenge the issue when Mr Grimes makes a positive statement that the site presented no archaeological problems to solve. There is according to Mr Gresley Jones no tittle of evidence produced by Mr Grimes to support such a categorical statement. Mr Grimes admitted to him that he could not account for the straight lines and rectangular nature of the design'. Yet it seems that North at least had done just that, by saying that the straight narrow lines are an illusion due to the angle of vision on approach, 'but at close quarters the lines resolve themselves into wide indefinite bands . . . The appearance of straight lines and right angles is an illusion resulting from the acuteness of the angle of vision consequent upon the low elevation of the observer, who will be standing in a rowing boat'. Grimes said much the same thing, in the *Weekly News* report:

> Looking from the distance some of the lines did look as though they might be those of a wall. Getting closer and examining them, you found that the formation was wide and shapeless, and I defy anyone to build any kind of wall out of the material which we found there.

Underwood added an opinion to the *Advertiser's* news report, pointing out that the 'experts' had made only a hurried examination of the site, and that those who had been there before over the years remained convinced 'that there is something behind the formation of the stones'. Both the papers' reporters say that the stones were observed for at least an hour, but Nigel Bannerman considers this impossible, saying they only had about twenty minutes. This is of course about the time people usually have, to see Llys Helig, but some, unlike North and Grimes, have done it more than once.

By December North had marshalled his arguments. The meeting of the Field Club at the Public Library then, which heard the official verdicts, was chaired by Willoughby Gardner. He opened it by saying that previous findings had tended to corroborate the legend, but indicated that the intention of this latest research would be final: it was carried out 'with the view of settling the matter for all time'. Grimes' paper was read in his absence. North was candid. He understood that it had been hoped that the August 17th expedition 'would have resulted in his having to eat his own words'. He had no intention of concurring with such a desire. He then set out his findings very much as they were eventually printed in the Field Club's 'Supplement to the Proceedings', in 1940, the document which has been frequently referred to in this book and which forms our principal source for North's views.

In the meantime, less than three weeks after the expedition, the world went to war, and Llys Helig was apparently forgotten for a further fifty-six years.

X The Bronze Age Coastline Project

Those who went on the 1995 trips told each other that they
were the first to approach the site with open minds, the first
not to be going there to prove or disprove a theory, but
simply to see what was there. They were investigating the
ancient coastline, as part of the 'Bronze Age Coastline
Project'. It was to be pure science.

They may have wanted to think that, but I do not think it
would be entirely possible. You cannot go to Llys Helig with
an open mind. You cannot go without being secretly a
believer or a sceptic in your heart.

The 'Bronze Age Coastline Project' was set up by Nigel
Bannerman in the early 1970's, initially intended to seek for
evidence of Bronze Age smelting sites. The trip to Llys Helig
was a part of this, not originally planned as any
investigation of the myth, and its lost palace. Through Dr
Cecil Jones, an archaeologist attached to Bangor University,
the trip came to the attention of Professor Dennis Wood,
who asked to come along. This was something of a
breakthrough, as Professor Wood was a highly-respected
authority on the geology of North Wales, internationally
recognised as pre-eminent in his field, and so perhaps the
best person available to comment on what was found.

Unusually the first trip of 1995 was in July, when a low
tide presented itself on the 14th and of course earlier
daylight assisted. Three boats left Deganwy at 5.30, one
however for some reason turning back before reaching the

target. Of those who got to the stones, Nigel Bannerman, leading the Project and the expedition, with Professor Dennis Wood and Dr Cecil Jones, went in an inflatable, some divers and a cartographer following. They reached the reef about 7.30, and the rocks were thoroughly examined both above and below water. The tide was not, apparently, the very lowest possible, so that a general overview of the site and its famous 'straight lines' could not have been possible. David Chapman dived on that occasion at the central angle of the zig-zag shape, then invisible under water but identifiable by the presence of a very large protruding rock. He tells me that he saw rounded beach stones, consistent with a geological feature, and nothing indicating the presence of anything other than beach material: no sign of walls or mortar, nothing to suggest any palace structure. It was like any other seabed, he says, the sort of thing you find in the debris field of an ice flow.

When Nigel Bannerman went that time he says that he initially didn't think there was anything there. He came away with much the same impression. The university scientists had taken numerous samples (randomly collected by the divers), and on the way one of those shifts took place which change, from time to time, the fashion in Llys Helig thinking. Professor Wood examined the samples, in the boat, and remarked that 'some of these stones are a bit too angular'. He said they looked as if they had been taken out to the site as building material. Unfortunately Professor Wood has since died, and the whereabouts of the samples is not known.

If stones were found on the Llys Helig reef which had demonstrably been shaped as for use in building, which is more than anyone at present claims, it would still of course not prove that there had been a building there. The reef, being foul ground, has been used for years as a dumping ground by the trawlers, which emptied the rubbish dredged in their nets there because it was not a place where they could fish. It is likely, but unproved, that cargo boats approaching Conwy would jettison their ballast there before entering the channel, the mouth of which occurs nearby, at the Fairway Buoy.

A second trip went out on 12th August, this time taking thirteen people in three boats. The usual dawn start from Deganwy got them to the site at 6.45. The tide was lower than in July. 'We were,' Marcus Elliott, one of the members of this expedition, tells me, 'walking around on dry land.' A photograph shows him doing so, with a broad scatter of revealed stones in the background. There is no pattern visible on any of the surface photographs, and in fact no reason to think that the reef is of any significant shape. They turned stones over, he tells me, looking for anything which might have been worked, but found nothing at all that looked like a cut stone.

Markers were laid to assist future surveys, and underwater photographs taken on this occasion probably point the way to future investigations, if such are felt worthwhile.

After the second trip it was clear that the next step would be to attempt a survey, but this had to wait until the next low tide, which was as far off as the spring of the following year.

In 1996, the greatest breakthrough in the history of the investigation of Llys Helig took place, when Nigel Bannerman succeeded in photographing it from the air. The lowest tide occurred on March 19th, and the day before markers were placed on the site to pinpoint it from the plane and measure it.

Two of the resulting slides show a shape in the water, lying to the south of the rocks of the reef itself. Although photographed through mist, and only in places protruding from the water, it is sufficiently identifiable to be described. It is a broad W in shape, two right-angles joined in the middle, the southern one longer and wider than its partner. This is familiar to us as Ashton's 'rectangular remains', the snaking lines of Horace Lees' photographs, indeed providing confirmation of his words: 'At the south extremity the wall turned abruptly at a right angle to the east, running quite straight for 100 or 120 yards. A further stretch of wall here met it in another right angle, running 40 yards south, and was continued a similar distance east again at another right angle.' We have to remember that for Lees the zig-zag appeared above water. The striking point is that his description perfectly fits the Bannerman aerial views.

It is a long way from the description of Grimes, who waded there, and so could not have seen a pattern if there had been one: 'I must insist that below water the stones extend over a wide area the limits of which I did not succeed in defining in any direction. I was left with the impression, not of a series of ridges which *might* have been ruined walls, but of an apparently unbroken mass of boulders . . . ' This ,it is true, was his impression; but he gained it from restricted observation. He was wrong, moreover, in saying at the Deganwy Castle meeting that he 'did not believe an aerial photograph would help in giving the shape of the mass'.

'DOOMED PALACE YIELDS SECRETS,' cried the *Weekly News*. 'Myth of Helig's watery grave: could it be true?' They published a plan of it based on Ashton's improvement of that of Horace Lees, which unfortunately does not conform to the definite W shape now seen from the air.

It is clear from the aerial photographs that there are two

distinct areas of Llys Helig: the broad reef to the north, some 100 metres long and no doubt tapering off indefinitely, as described by Grimes; and the zig-zag shape about 100 metres to its south, extending over an area of perhaps 170 metres. No-one claims the former to contain right angles or defined straight lines, so there is little point in discovering that it includes no apparent worked stones. It is the second feature, clearly, which is shown in the Lees photographs, and dramatically described by Ashton.

A common error, it seems, is the confusion of the two. It seems that on the more recent visits the rectilinear shape now known to exist did not show above water. Indeed one wonders if it has appeared clearly at all since Lees and Ashton saw it.

The photographs apparently also showed a semi-circular mark lying to the north of the W, which of course it was tempting to see as the base of the speculated 'tower', though personally I would judge the impression on the slide to be too faint to base on that any confident statement. Also shown, this time more definitely, is a more or less straight line veering away from the site to the west, which is no doubt the well-established feature known as St Seiriol's causeway.

Plans were laid for a further attempt the following year. Photographs were now taken by the survey team of other sites along the coast as well as Llys Helig, such as the medieval fish weirs in the Menai Strait. These, Nigel Bannerman says, lie 'on the same submarine contour'. Their present location below normal low water, revealed, like Llys Helig, at exceptional tides, indicates a change in sea level over perhaps the last eight hundred years. They would not be functional as fish-traps now.

This is not, however, anything like the forty foot

difference which North said would be necessary to place ancient Llys Helig on dry land. Nigel Bannerman points out that since our maximum tidal range, in these coastal waters, of twenty-seven feet, actually reveals Llys Helig now and then, something much less than a difference of forty feet would be required to put it above water.

Cadw, the Welsh Heritage governing body, undertook a 'Coastal fish weir survey', which, together with a Coastal Erosion Survey, identified over twenty weirs within Gwynedd, and the likelihood of many more. 'The walls of the weirs may be constructed of stone, or stakes with wattle woven between them, or a combination of the two.' There is little or no evidence, they tell us on the website, 'for weirs in Wales dating from before Medieval times', and they cite the reference from the *Hanes Taliesin* concerning 'Gored Wyddno', in its Cardigan Bay version. 'Dates of the 10th century have been obtained from traps in the Severn Estuary, and Prehistoric dates are known from Denmark.'

Similarly the Clwyd Coastal Survey discovered evidence of medieval fishing in the form of two substantial stone and timber fishing weirs, or 'goradau', marked by boulders and stakes on the beach at Rhos-on-Sea.

The 'medieval' date given for these features is often an assumption, based partly on a sketchy knowledge of historic tide levels and an apparent monastic connection in the location of the sites, and firm dates for any of them (relying on the discovery of datable, and stratified, material) have yet to be produced. In any case as the materials were presumably continually renewed over centuries a piece of wood incorporated in them would tell us little about the age of the weir. In some cases however the 'medieval' date is fully justified since fishing weirs were of such importance that they occur in deeds and charters and in the sheriffs' and bailiffs' accounts forming the assessments of rents.

Though some of these fish weirs are curved in a broad semi-circle (though too large, of course, ever to be mistaken for the bases of towers) the characteristic and striking shape of some of them, such as the one off the monastic settlement at Llanfaes, is that of a distinct V. The shape under water at Llys Helig in the aerial photographs, and the right-angled lines sometimes revealed and photographed above the surface, is therefore consistent with being two such fish-traps side by side.

The analogy with known fish weirs is useful. The one at Gogarth, just off the Great Orme, is only visible at extreme low tide; but two at Deganwy, near the 'Black Rocks' and so just off the point where Castell Tremlyd once stood, may be seen at moderate lows.

One of these has already been referred to. They are known by names which bring us centuries back to the story of Elffin, in some, perhaps the more authentic, versions placed specifically in Conwy Bay. 'Gorad' is a common local Welsh term for these features, more correctly 'Gored', mutated from the Welsh word *cored* meaning 'a weir'; and the outer one of this pair, a long curved line, is known as Gorad Faelgwn, after King Maelgwn, the Dark Age ruler of Gwynedd whose seat was on the Vardre nearby, who became associated with Elffin's tale. This is the 'great weir of Gannow', as part of Deganwy was called, giving us the name Gannock, which records subsequently tell us 'was called Goret Vailgon', held during the middle ages by the three vills of the eastern bank, 'Ganneu', 'Bodescathlan', and 'Penlassoc', which split between them equally the forty shillings a year at which the weir had been valued in the 'Extent of the County of Caernarvon' drawn up for Edward I in 1284. So at least I gather from H.R. Davies' work published in *The Conway and the Menai Ferries*.

The other fish weir at Deganwy is called Gorad Wyddno. The 1849 Guidebook to Llandudno referred to it as if it had been fairly recently in use. Maelgwn's brother Gwyddno, 'the Lord of Cantref Gwaelod, a hundred in Merionethshire, since overflowed by the sea, resided some time in the neighbourhood. The latter had near his residence a weir, called Gored Wyddno (*Gwyddno's Weir*) which is even yet known by the same name, and belongs to the Hon. Mr Mostyn, as owner of the house of Bodscallan. This weir is often mentioned in the ancient British writings as the most productive of any in the country . . . ' Since its ownership must have had some significance we may suppose that the occupants of Bodysgallen at one time caught their salmon there.

At Rhos Fynach, the ancient monastic site at Rhos-on-Sea, such a working fish weir survived into recent enough times to have provided some fine photographic records. These show the characteristic long sharp V, formed of a base of rounded stones, with a tall superstructure of stakes interwoven with wattle. A second former weir near the pier at Rhos had gone by the last quarter of the 19th century. The Rhos Fynach weir had belonged to Aberconwy Abbey in the late 12th century, and when the abbey was removed to Maenan in 1289 it fell into the ownership of the Earl of Leicester, as Lord of Denbigh, until 1575 when it passed into private ownership, being, when Bezant Lowe published in the first volume of his *Heart of Northern Wales* in 1912, owned by a Mr William Horton, J.P., of Bryn Dinarth, who had bought it from a descendant of the man to whom the Earl of Leicester had granted it.

It is perhaps significant that fish weirs had become illegal by the Salmon Law of 1860, unless they could show a title back as far as the reign of James I. Rhos Fynach survived an enquiry, a tribute to its documentation, but many such weirs were demolished at that time.

Of course, as a writer quoted by Bezant Lowe points out, the weir was constantly renewed: 'This skilful piece of human ingenuity has withstood the storms of eight centuries, and, though none of the original material remains, it still retains its "form".'

Gorad Wyddno, like Rhos Fynach, is of the long V-shaped form. Seen at almost eye level, sticking out of the sea, it looks remarkably like the long straight lines which meet at a right-angle in the classic photographs of Llys Helig.

XI Elffin's Weir

Let us for a moment, and for the first time in this book,
indulge in speculation. Let us assume that the origin of the
Llys Helig rocks is purely geological. It was not a Dark Age
king who put them there, but a melting glacier. Let us
assume that the scattered rocks are partly a denuded
drumlin, a lump of matter left by the ice flow at its extremity
since washed bare by the sea. We know that this must once,
or perhaps several times, over the course of the multiple
millennia, have stood on dry land, and that at least one such
occasion occurred during times when people might have
lived on this coastal plain, then submerged by a rising sea. It
is perfectly possible, as we have seen, that a memory of the
loss of the lands around it could have survived in tradition,
and become moulded into the form of an old tale. But the
connection of loss by inundation with Llys Helig need not
stop there.

If the debris of the ice flow lay at a point, at one time,
near low water, it could have been put to use as a fish weir.
Glacial moraine at Deganwy, Gogarth, Llanfaes and
elsewhere certainly and visibly was. If this is what occurred
and what explains the regular rectilinear forms, then it
seems likely that 'Gorad Llys Helig' would have been an
important and valuable asset to whoever controlled it.
Perhaps, like the weir bequeathed by Gwyddno to his son
Elffin, the most productive in the land. As a result it would
be likely also to have had associated structures, secure fish

handling and housing buildings, and even human dwellings where a permanent presence representing the owner could monitor and protect its catches. The sight of all that going beneath a relentless sea, whether gradually or by some sudden freak event, would inevitably leave its own indelible memory.

The myth and the geological and historic background are thus, in the end, compatible. Though it probably was not the palace of a king, it possibly was a place of important human activity. Though we have no certain evidence of this, as yet, we certainly, from the visible shape of the angled lines and the comparison with other *goradau*, have reason to surmise it; and at the very least we have no ground to rule it out.

The myth is thus saved, either way, for those who wish to preserve it. Some would like to find evidence of a sudden catastrophic inundation; some would be happy to find simply datable material. Neither of these types of data has yet been found – though the search goes on.

I would have liked to be able to say at this point that I had some first-hand evidence to help me in the matter of the factual identity of Llys Helig. This season there were low enough tides in August and September, but the weather was against it, as it has so often humbugged and restricted investigators before. It hardly needs to be said by now that it is extremely difficult to view Llys Helig. For one thing it is a long way away from your likely starting point, Deganwy beach. Though Penmaenmawr is nearer, the prospect of dragging a boat across such a distance of soft sand has deterred most people. You have to leave Deganwy before the channel dries out, then wait for an hour or so for Llys Helig to appear. If there is an onshore breeze or indeed any turbulent water you have wasted your time: the tide's massing will partly submerge the reef, even at the point at which it surfaces. Add to this the inconvenient hour, the rarity of the critical tides – since even a few feet can make the difference between seeing the rocks or the seaweed – and one can see why only a relatively few people have actually been there.

You can, however, see Llys Helig from land. Both Moel Llys, above Trwyn yr Wylfa, and Allt Wen, the other wing of the valley which shelters Dwygyfylchi, overlook its patch of sea.

Allt Wen is a south-westerly extension of Conwy Mountain, and the site of a hill-fort which must have been an outpost of the greater one there. The approach to the summit is so steep that its slope blocks your view of what is beyond, so that even when you actually come onto its top through the upper rampart and cross the narrow citadel to look out the other side you can still only guess what, if anything, you will see. I find myself when now about to see Llys Helig for the first time, or perhaps not, experiencing a sort of apprehension. What will it be like? Will it be strange, or perhaps even ominous?

You are very much alone, at first light on Allt Wen. Everything is diminished by distance, and as the day breaks over the Carneddau and light spreads across the slopes of mountains, at an hour when even the farm dogs are still asleep, you are not in the normal world.

What do I see? I see the constant sea breaking over a distant coastal reef. The sight, as I might have expected, provides more questions than answers. There are many such reefs of stones around our coasts. Why am I bewitched into writing about this one?

Llys Helig emerges hesitantly, as if cautiously, like a badger from its sett. Then when it finally comes, it comes quickly. Half an hour before low water a clutch of dark boulders breaks the surface. A few minutes later there is something definitely mistakable for a straight line. Then two quite close parallel lines. One thing one begins to feel about it is that it is not a distinguished or impressive feature. Not, for instance, like the great black sprawl of its neighbour, Caer Gonwy, a glacial deposit slightly more inland and directly under Conwy Mountain, which impressive feature I could see to my right on the way up. Why, one wonders, did the legend not get attached to that phenomenon, much more easily seen, a much more striking outcrop? The sheer insignificance (at least from this distance and angle) of the Llys Helig reef, makes all the more a demand to explain the attachment to this reclusive and imposing outcrop, of the powerful, indeed compelling, legend.

Up on that hilltop that pale autumn morning, it must be said that I did come to a conclusion. Given all the many reasons for *not* attaching to Llys Helig this ancient story – indeed for not even being aware of Llys Helig at all – the only credible explanation for the improbable association of the story with the rocks is that, at least in some way, the story is true.

Conscious of sitting inside an Iron Age hillfort, I have the odd experience of feeling repeatedly, as I look through my telescope, that there is somebody behind me. I find myself looking compulsively over my shoulder, though I know there can be no-one else on the mountains at that hour. I find myself walking to the other edge of the outlook, to confirm that no-one is approaching. Is this something about the fact I am in a hillfort? Can it be that a fear of intrusion, a suspicion of strangers, could get somehow fixed into the physical makeup of a place?

Yet even in such an apparently susceptible state of mind I see nothing about the reef of Llys Helig, through my binoculars, through my field telescope on its tripod, or with the naked eye, except the interminable heave of waves forever breaking on it. I am aware of nothing about it, seeing it, except its distance, and its apparent insignificance. I sense more a feeling of the suffocating sea.

No doubt some summer mornings of still water, after all necessarily at slack tide, the reef could be quiescent. I know that people have walked on it on calm days, and people have dived there in still water. My own view of it happens to include an onshore breeze, no gale but just enough to embed in my vision around it the surge and swell of the sea.

Today, although the tide is the lowest, there are definitely no zig-zag shapes visible – perhaps because the tide level is raised by the onshore breakers. What I see is the highest members of the reef of stones itself.

Almost as soon as the tide turns the waves start to wash over the tops of Llys Helig's stones again. Half an hour after low water it is practically gone. When it goes again it evaporates quickly, as if in a few minutes. That massive tide pours in, much as it did for Helig, until it is a matter of waves breaking over largely hidden rocks, cold in the dawn light, white on grey. Then it is gone.

I came back to Allt Wen and the distant view of Llys Helig twelve hours later, as the light faded on a misty evening and clouds covered the nearby hills and threatened my composure. The light falling from the other hemisphere threw a silver sheen across the bay. The waves continued to pester the reef. It was strange to be in this unusual place at both the first and the last light of the day.

What has this double experience given me? How has it added to my relationship with Llys Helig?

Well, it has made Llys Helig more mysterious to me, after actually seeing it, rather than less. It has reinforced the feeling I had of it from the start, that there are more things unknown about it than will ever be known. That is not to say that we might not have, in this book, unravelled the enigma of what it actually is. What I think we can never quite pin down, and log as data, is what it means.

In every way the sea dominates the idea, as well as the reality, of Helig ap Glannog and his court. Surfacing from it with so much constraint imposed, for periods of minutes rather than hours, perhaps three times each year if you are lucky, what chance has Helig got, in history, against the sea?

I suppose that he has this one: we are still writing about him, centuries later. I and many others still get drawn back to his decadent court, where we want to hear the harpist play.

You feel that this cannot be entirely accidental, and that whatever other lack of evidence there may be, there is the evidence of our own repeated fascination, a facet of the durability of the myth. Such enduring images could not get attached so firmly to a coastal reef for no reason. If this were only a glacial deposit, and nothing more, I cannot now help feeling, I would not be writing about it, nor you reading.

There is the fact too that whatever it may originally have been, it has for some considerable time borne the name of Helig, and it is today, at least in its role of carrying through time his memory, Helig's court.

Bibliography

Chapter I
ASHTON, W. *The Evolution of a Coastline*, Edward Standford Ltd., London, 1920.

NORTH, F.J. *The Legend of Llys Helig – its origin and its significance*. Llandudno, Colwyn Bay & District Field Club supplement to proceedings, Llandudno, 1940.

RHYS, Sir J. *Celtic Folklore*. Oxford University Press, 1901.

LOWE, W.B. (ed.) *An Ancient Survey of Penmaenmawr*, 1906.

Chapter II
NORTH, F.J. *Sunken Cities*. University of Wales Press, 1955.

Chapter III
STEPHENS, M. *The Oxford Companion to the Literature of Wales*. Oxford University Press.

SMITH, M. (ed.) *The Triads of Britain*. Wildwood House Ltd., 1977.

FOX, Sir C. & DICKENS, B. (eds.) *The Early Cultures of North-West Europe*, Cambridge University Press, 1950.

JONES, G. & T. (trs. & eds.) *The Mabinogion*. Dent (Everyman), 1957.

GUEST, Lady C. (trs. & ed.) *The Mabinogion*. Dent (Everyman), 1906.

FORD, P.J. (trs. & ed.) *The Mabinogi, and other Medieval Welsh tales*. University of California Press, 1977.

Chapter IV
DAWSON SCOTT, C.A. *Nooks & Corners of Cornwall*. London, Eveleigh Nash, undated.

SAVAGE, A. (trs & ed.) *The Anglo-Saxon Chronicles*. Book Club Associates, 1983.

CRAWFORD, O.G.S. *Lyonesse*, in *Antiquity I*. 1 March 1927.

VINAVER, E. (ed.) *The Works of Sir Thomas Malory*. Clarendon Press, Oxford, 1967.

WILLIAMS P. (trs.), LE CUNFF. *Brittany*, Oest France, undated.

Brittany, Michelin Guide.

DANIEL, G. *The Megalith Builders of Western Europe*. Pelican, 1962.

PENNANT, T. *Tours in Wales*. Humphreys, Caernarvon, 1883.

MORANT, P. *The History and Antiquity of the Coast of Essex*. 1763.

Chapter V
INNES, M.M. (trs. & ed.) OVID, *Metamorphoses*. Penguin, 1975.

LATTIMORE, R. (trs. & ed.) *The Odes of Pindar*. University of Chicago Press, 1971.

KIRK, G.S. *The Nature of Greek Myths*. Penguin, 1974.

KIRK, G.S. *Myth, its Meaning and Function in Ancient and other Cultures*. Cambridge University Press, 1970.

OPPENHEIM, A.L. *Ancient Mesopotamia*. University of Chicago Press, 1964.

SANDARS, N.K. (trs. & ed.) *The Epic of Gilgamesh*. Penguin, 1960.

JORDAN, M. *Myths of the World*. Kyle Cathie Ltd., 1993.

YOUNG, J.J. (trs. & ed.) *The Prose Edda*. Bowes & Bowes, 1954.

DAVIDSON, H.R.E. *Gods and Myths of Northern Europe*. Pelican, 1964.

CAVENDISH, R. *Mythology, an illustrated encyclopaedia*. Orbis, 1980.

GOETZ, D. & MORLEY, S.G. (trs. & eds.) *Popol Vuh*. University of Oklahoma Press, 1950.

OSBORNE, H. *South American Mythology*. Newnes Books, 1968.

SENIOR, M. *Who's Who in Mythology*. Orbis, 1985.

Chapter VI
MARINATOS, Sp. *Some Words about the Legends of Atlantis*. Athens, 1971.

MARINATOS, Sp. *The Volcanic Destruction of Minoan Crete*, in *Antiquity*, Vol. XIII. 52, December 1939.

INCE, J.V. *The End of Atlantis – New Light on an Old Legend*. Paladin, 1969.

HANCOCK, G. *Fingerprints of the Gods*. Book Club Associates & William Heinemann, 1995.

Chapter VII
ASHE, G. *From Caesar to Arthur*. Collins, 1960.

JACKSON, K. *The International Popular Tale and Early Welsh Tradition*. University of Wales Press, 1961.

SENIOR, M. *Myths of Britain*. Orbis, 1979.

CHADWICK, N. *The British Heroic Age*. University of Wales Press, 1976.

Chapter VIII

STEERS, J.A. *The Coastline of England and Wales*. Cambridge University Press, 1946.

REID MOIR, J. two papers in *The Journal of the Royal Anthropological Institute*, Vol. LI, 1921; Vol. LV, 1925.

GRANT, M. (trs. & ed.) *Tacitus: The Annals of Imperial Rome*. Penguin, 1981.

MATTINGLY, H. (trs. & ed.) *Tacitus on Britain and Germany*. Penguin, 1965.

LLOYD, Sir J. *A History of Wales*. Longman, 1939.

GIRALDUS CAMBRENSIS *The Itinerary Through Wales*. Dent (Everyman), 1908.

McDONALD, G.L. *Tidal Aggression*, in *The Seafarer*, Summer 2001.

Chapter IX

PARRY, T. *Llys Helig*. Coastline Publications, 1996.

Chapter X

BANNERMAN, N. *Bronze Age Coast Project, Llys Helig 1997*. Private paper.

LOWE, W.B. *The Heart of Northern Wales*. Vol. I. Llanfairfechan, 1912.

DAVIES, H.R. *The Conway and the Menai Ferries*. University of Wales Press, 1966.